T0382246

Per Mollerup
Simplicity: A Matter of Design

Per Mollerup
Simplicity: A Matter of Design

BIS Publishers
Building Het Sieraad
Postjesweg 1
1057 DT Amsterdam
The Netherlands
T-31 (0)20 515 02 30
F-31 (0)20 515 02 39
bis@bispublishers.nl
www.bispublishers.nl

ISBN 978-90-6369-402-9

Design Per Mollerup

Thanks
Margot og Thorvald Dreyers Fond (Copenhagen)
has generously supported the research for
Simplicity: A Matter of Design.

?!
**The cover motif is a verbatim account of an alleged
exchange of cables between French author Victor Hugo
and his publisher** (see p150).

Simple is *never* that simple.
Jerry Levov in Philip Roth:
American Pastoral, 1997, p68

Contents

Introduction
The ultimate design factor

Simplicity is the ultimate design factor, that single quality which more than anything else is sought in design, by designers and by users. Simplicity is indeed a matter of design.

As the world becomes increasingly complex and complicated, simplicity becomes increasingly in demand. We all seek simplicity in small or large measure. We strive to create simplicity at work and at home. For short or long periods of our lives we may opt for some kind of simple life as relief from a complex everyday.

While the lives of our early ancestors may appear simple to us, it would not be simple for us to live those lives. We wouldn't know how to cope with that kind of simplicity. We have forgotten the virtues that made the life of our ancestors possible. To us, the simple life of the past would be extremely complicated. This takes us to the root of simplicity: simplicity is not an absolute quality. It depends on our experience, knowledge, understanding, and skills.

Simplicity, complexity, and complication are qualities found everywhere: in nature and in the human-made world. Scientists look for the simple beauty behind the complex surface. Inventors, engineers, and designers work hard to simplify processes and products. We all seek simple explanations, patterns that let us understand the world, natural or human-made. We like to think that behind every complexity there is simplicity waiting to be discovered. But behind that simplicity, another layer of complexity may lurk.

Design is a spectator sport, but there is more to it than meets the eye. Simplicity in design concerns aesthetics, functionality, and ethics as experienced by visual and other appreciation, by use, and by contemplation. *Simplicity: A Matter of Design* explores and describes.

Figure 1
Safety pin, aka baby pin
Invention Walter Hunt, 1849
The problem of attaching or binding something temporarily has inspired several brilliantly simple designs such as buttons, pins, snap fasteners, zippers, Velcro, and Post-it.

Nomen est numen, we must name the thing to think about it. Linguistic variation enables precise thinking and communication. Special fields of knowledge tend to have special vocabularies. Not so with simplicity. Simplicity in design has long suffered from absence of a precise vocabulary that divides the monolithic word *simple* into a number of *simples* that describe different colours of simplicity.

Linguistic relativity suggests that the structure of a language affects the ways in which its users conceptualise their world; it determines, or at least influences, their cognitive processes. Here we suggest that introduction of a few new terms may improve thinking about simplicity in design. *Simplicity: A Matter of Design* offers a set of terms that will allow us to discuss simplicity in design with precision.

First, we will distinguish between *complex* and *complicated,* two words that in daily parlance and in most of the literature are used synonymously, but stimulate good thinking if used with semantic distance. This idea is not new, although not universally accepted.

Second, we will split the monolithic *simple,* the antonym of both complex and complicated, into two words, one contrasting complex and one contrasting complicated.

Third, we will distinguish between simplicity, which can be experienced immediately, and simplicity which presupposes some learning before it can be enjoyed.

The perspective of this book is obviously the designer's, which is anything but narrow. Out of the ivory tower, the designer takes his natural point of departure in the user's situation – with due respect to production, distribution, and global husbandry.

Per Mollerup
Melbourne and Copenhagen, 2015

This chapter addresses fundamental questions concerning simplicity in design: what is it? Where is it? Why is it? How is it?

Simplicity appears to be so simple a concept that nobody cares to define its exact meaning. That is perhaps fine in everyday language. However, when talking seriously about simplicity in design, we must know what exactly the term stands for. *Simplicity* stands for a lot of different things. Some semantic filtering is needed. Which meanings are relevant to design?

Edward de Bono
An expert is someone who has succeeded in making decisions and judgements simpler through knowing what to pay attention to and what to ignore.

Robert Greenberg
The challenge is about taking things that are definitely complex and making them simpler and more understandable.

Bruno Munari
Progress means simplicity, not complicating.

Antoine de St. Exupery
If anything at all, perfection is finally attained not when there is no longer anything to add, but when there is no longer anything to take away.

Lao Tzu
I have just three things to teach: simplicity, patience, compassion. These three are your greatest treasures.

Alfred North Whitehead
Seek simplicity and distrust it.

Erik Christopher Zeeman
Technical skill is mastery of complexity, while creativity is mastery of simplicity.

The quotes here and at the following chapter starts show the extent to which simplicity has occupied great minds – with varying results. The quotes do not necessarily align with our principles.

Simplicity means *the quality of being simple. Simple* means *not complex or complicated. Simple* also has several other meanings irrelevant to our inquiry.

Complex and *complicated* have neighbouring meanings and are often used synonymously. Nevertheless there can be interesting nuances in the usage of the two expressions.

In its nuanced meaning, *complex* stands for *consisting of connected parts.* This is a quantitative, objective property. It can be observed and counted. Complexity is part of the object. No matter which user looks at the object, it will have the same number of connected parts.

In its nuanced meaning, *complicated* stands for *difficult to understand.* This is a qualitative, subjective property. Complication depends on the abilities of the user. To some users, the object may be complicated; to others, it may be simple.

Taking the nuanced meanings of *complex* and *complicated* into consideration we could define simple as *not consisting of connected parts and not difficult to understand.*

As the first part of this definition will exclude any item consisting of two or more connected parts, we will soften it to align it with common understanding of the word *simple* and at the same time remove the negations: *simple* means

> *consisting of relatively few connected parts and being easy to understand.*

The term *relatively few parts* suggests a comparison with the observer's expectations, a fact that adds an element of subjectivity to the first part of the definition. The second part of the definition describes a truly subjective property.

Dictionaries offer several definitions of *complex* and *complicated.* The definitions presented in *Simplicity: A Matter of Design* are in line with definitions found in *Oxford English Dictionary:*

*Complex, adj.
Consisting of or comprehending various parts united or connected together; formed by combination of different elements; composite, compound. Said of things, ideas, etc.*

*Complicated, adj.
Consisting of an intimate combination of parts or elements not easy to unravel or separate; involved, intricate, confused.*

The subjectivity of simplicity matches our common understanding. A simple equation of second degree may be totally complicated to a person who never learned maths.

As mentioned previously, our daily use of the words *complex* and *complicated* is not completely stringent. We say that a lamp is complicated if we have to loosen a great number of screws to change the bulb, even if the construction is easy to understand. *Complex* would, in principle, be the correct term, as it is the number of parts, not the understandability, that is the problem. However, *complicated* is often used to describe processes that, however simple to understand, are burdensome and take some time.

Summing up: simplicity is both an objective and (most often) a subjective property. Simplicity is very much in the mind of the beholder.

2

Figure 2
PK14 armchair, 1962
Design Poul Kjærholm
Manuf. E. Kold Christensen,
Denmark
Simple does not equal low price. Simplicity often has a price. The PK14 armchair of dull chromium-plated steel and ox hide is undeniably simple, but simplification has been used to make an exclusive rather than cheap product.

**The word *design* designates both the process
and the result of shaping all kinds of tools. All
man-made objects with a practical purpose are
tools. They make our life possible, easy, and
interesting. Intention, material, and technology
define the field where tools are created. Intention
represents our wants, while material and
technology stand for possibilities and constraints
in the process and its result. New materials and
new technologies give way to new processes
and new results. Needs, wants, and scarcity of
resources inspire new technology.**

3

**Tools are made by using other tools. The first
human-made tools were made by using 'tools'
found in nature: mineral, animal, and vegetable.
Later, human-made tools were made by using
other human-made tools. For obvious reasons the
first generations of human-made tools were simple
tools. Primitive humans didn't start by making an
adjustable wrench or a mobile phone. How could
they? Why would they?**

**Early tools had simple functions and simple
shapes. A pair of primitive wool shears is little
more than a bent piece of iron with two sharp
edges. Hand-operated wool shears were probably
invented in the Iron Age and were refined and used
for thousands of years before being replaced by
electric shears.**

**In terms of technology, electric wool shears
are complex tools compared with hand shears.
In terms of use, the process of shearing sheep
has become a simpler affair. This reflects one of
the main reasons for designing new tools and
developing new technology: new tools and new
technologies make life easier, in a word: simpler.
Simplicity for the user is a purposive element in
good design. The simplicity is typically enabled by
complex tools.**

Figure 3
**Wool shears
Manuf. Keiser, USA**
Early tools were simple tools.
A pair of blade shears is
basically a bent piece of iron
with two sharp edges. In cold
climates blade shears are still
preferred to machine shears
as they leave some wool on
the sheep.
Rather than becoming
obsolete, old technology
often acquires a more
specialised use when new
technology is introduced.

Our forefathers and foremothers lived a simple life. Few will contest this. And few will deny that their descendants developed a vast array of tools, each of which simplified some practical function or another. Nevertheless, many feel that life today is more complex than ever. How did this happen?

Simplicity is not just simplicity. It happens on several levels.

The simplicity experienced by our early ancestors was mental, as choices were fewer. On a physical level, life was not that simple. It was demanding. Life was a fight for food and for shelter. The simplicity of poverty implies physical burdens and demands physical skills and efforts.

The simplicity enabled by the avalanche of modern technology is physical. Today, few of us in the developed world fight for food or shelter. Division of labour, specialisation, and technological development have made our lives quite easy, quite simple physically. At the same time, our lives have become quite taxing on the mental level: so many choices, so much to know, to understand, and to respond to. The simplicity of affluence implies mental burdens, and demands mental skills and efforts.

Mental loads have accompanied our relief from physical burdens.

Simplicity is an option in the design of all kinds of artefacts: tools and appliances, visual communications, buildings, towns, systems, processes, and other human accomplishments.

We curse the complicated home entertainment system. It should be simpler for non-technicians to install and operate. The written instructions are complicated, too. The technicians who wrote them probably understand everything technical, but can't imagine how difficult home entertainment systems can be to laypeople. Appliances can be complicated or simple, and so can communications.

Workplaces, office buildings, hospitals, airports, freeway junctions, and many other human-made environments are sometimes sheer mazes, yet without the charm of such time-honoured mazes as Venice or the Kasbah of Marrakech.

We have problems completing our income tax form, partly because of the design of the form, partly because of the underlying system. Communications can be complicated or simple, and so can the underlying system, the subject being communicated: railway networks, accounting systems, organisations, hospitals, political bodies, and more.

Production processes can also be simple or complicated. It is simpler to fry an egg than to make a crème brûlée. The crème brûlée can be made in more or less simple ways. Great industrial advances build on new technologies that in some respects simplify the production process.

Simplicity: A Matter of Design focuses on physical objects and visual communications: tools for doing and tools for thinking. The visual communications discussed concern contents that in turn can be simple or not.

Figure 4
**Azuma House,
Osaka, Japan, 1976
Design Tadao Ando**
Architecture is one of many fields where simplicity can be an important quality of the result.
The simple facade of Azuma House represents an ingeniously organised house sliced in between two other buildings on a 65 m² site. One of Tadao Ando's very first buildings.

4

Being the antonym of both complexity and complication, simplicity is both an objective and a subjective quality.

Most of the time complexity and complication relate as cause and effect. *A large work is difficult because it is large,* said Dr Johnson *. Most times, complexity increases complication. But sometimes, complexity decreases complication. A simple example explains how: a watch dial without figures or strokes appears simpler, but is less simple to read than a watch dial with figures or strokes. This is confusing. The problem resides partly in the language. While we distinguish between *complex* and *complicated* these words share one antonym: *simple.*

*Preface to *A Dictionary of the English Language*, 1755

A more articulate language would split the monolithic *simple* into two *simples* with the necessary semantic distance. One *simple* would stand for the opposite of complex; the other *simple* would stand for the opposite of complicated.

We will distinguish between *quantity-simple* and *quality-simple* as the opposites of *complex* and *complicated,* respectively. The empty watch dial is quantity-simple, but complicated (to read). The watch dial with numbers is complex, but quality-simple. In *Simplicity: A Matter of Design* we shall only use the bulky terms *quantity-simple* and *quality-simple* when needed to avoid confusion. In all other situations we shall use the monolithic *simple.*

We don't propose, save expect, that *quantity-simple* and *quality-simple* will enter everyday language, but certainly recommend these terms for professional design discourse.

Another factor, apart from vocabulary, adding to confusion is that we compare apples with pears when we hold the simple *appearance* against the complicated *readability*. Different attributes have different qualities. When talking about the practical use of a watch, quality-simplicity, easy understandability, is the interesting concept. When considering the watch as a piece of jewellery, quantity-simplicity, elegant appearance, becomes relevant.

Figure 5–8
OM4 watch, 1965
OM1 watch, 1962
OM2 watch, 1962
OM3 watch, 1962
**Design Ole Mathiesen
Manuf. Ole Mathiesen,
Denmark**
Which of these four watches is most simple in terms of appearance and readability?

5

6

7

8

**Complexity is humankind's modern context. If
we want to reap the benefits of modern society,
complexity is an intrinsic part of the deal. The trick is
to limit the complication that so easily follows from
complexity.**

**In his book, *Living with Complexity*, Donald A.
Norman discusses our need for complexity. He
rightly states that complexity is a fact of the world,
while complication is a state of mind. However,
Living with Complexity has been presented as an
attack on simplicity. That is a 50 per cent wrong
conclusion caused by the missing distinction
between quantity-simplicity and quality-simplicity.
Accepting complexity does not necessarily mean
defying simplicity. It is a matter of design to
domesticate complexity by quality-simple solutions:
to make products with complex content easy to
understand and use.**

Norman, Donald A.
Living with Complexity
MIT Press, Cambridge, MA,
2010

A design can be
– complex and quality-simple
– complex and complicated
– quantity-simple and quality-simple
– quantity-simple and complicated

**The diagram below exemplifies these four
possibilities:**

	QUALITY-SIMPLE	COMPLICATED
COMPLEX	A watch with numbers is complex, a matter of appearance, and quality-simple, a matter of understanding	Most VCRs are both complex, a matter of appearance, and complicated, a matter of understanding
QUANTITY SIMPLE	A paperclip is both quantity-simple, a matter of appearance, and quality-simple, a matter of understanding,	A watch without numbers or strokes is quantity-simple, a matter of appearance, and complicated, a matter of understanding.

9

The simplicity of a tool is to a high degree a subjective quality that depends on the competencies of the user. In turn these competencies may depend on the user's practical experiences with the tool in question and similar tools. Tools are simpler to the experienced user than to the beginner. Quality-simplicity is an advantage of scale. The more we practise, the easier the work becomes. *Simplicity favours the prepared mind*, to paraphrase Louis Pasteur. The problem is that in many cases we never get the critical experience, because we only meet the situation once or a few times in our lifetime. We remain beginners. Tools to be handled by beginners should be designed with this in mind.

Sometimes users don't have time to learn; they must understand and act intuitively. This is the case in many emergency situations, sometimes with lives at stake. In other situations with less stress users may not find it worthwhile to enter a longer learning curve, because the situation probably will not appear again. On the other hand, there are many situations where users are prepared to invest the necessary time and effort to learn something so well that they will find it simple. For most of us it is OK to use days learning to type. Novice smartphone owners also find it worthwhile to take a couple of hours to become acquainted with the device.

It is the designer's responsibility to balance a new device's learning requirements with the user's expected frequency of use and willingness to learn. The choice is between *general simplicity*, which means instant simplicity, and *special simplicity*, which means simplicity dependent on learning. An ideal keyboard for a person who will use a keyboard only once in a lifetime would be a keyboard with the letters in alphabetical order (provided the person is literate). That is general simplicity. For users familiar with typing, a standard QWERTY keyboard would be preferable. That is special simplicity. General and special simplicity are relative concepts dependent on the user's competencies. In both cases we talk about quality-simplicity.

Figure 10
iPhone, 2008
Design Jonathan Ive
Manuf. Apple, USA

Figure 11
BlackBerry 8110 Smartphone,
2006/2007
Design Jason Griffin /
Cortez Corley / Todd Wood
Manuf. RIM, Canada

Figure 10–11
The QWERTY pattern was originally designed to prevent the type bars on a mechanical typewriter from colliding and jamming. The means was to locate letters that often followed each other far away from one another on the keypad. As a lucky side effect this also enabled faster typing. The QWERTY pattern is maintained in many modern devices like the iPhone where there are no type bars that can collide. The BlackBerry mobile phone with SureType features two letters on each key, but is still organised as QWERTY.
Both phones are based on special simplicity. They presuppose elementary typing skills.

10

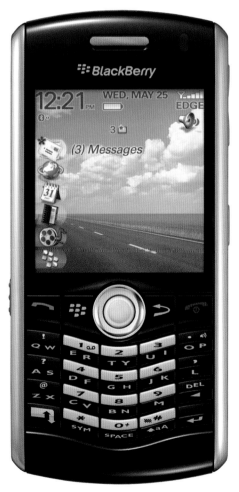

11

Simplicity in designing artefacts can be intentional or be imposed by a lack of technology or resources. When intentional, we seek simplicity with one or more motives in mind.

Functionality is the obvious and most common motive for seeking simplicity in design. Simple solutions are easier to deal with than complicated solutions. This applies to physical objects, and to communication. It is easier to operate a simple photocopier than a complicated photocopier. If we need written user instructions, we prefer simple instructions to complicated instructions. We hate instructions that require instructions: *How to read these instructions*. When the word *simple* refers to functionality, it means *easy to use*. This can be a question of quality-simplicity as well as of quantity-simplicity. To change the car's wheels can be difficult to comprehend and laborious too.

Aesthetics is a second motive for simplicity. Aesthetes often prefer simple solutions to complex solutions. They simply find simple solutions more attractive. When the word *simple* refers to aesthetics, it means *minimalist*. This is a question of quantity-simplicity.

Ethics is a third motive for seeking simplicity. Followers of religious movements, citizens with social convictions, people with environmental conscience, and many other thoughtful people seek simplicity for moral reasons. They prefer little to much. Other people have similar preferences because they think that too many possessions compromise a good life. When the word *simple* refers to ethics, it can, as a rule, be substituted by *austere*. This is a question of quantity-simplicity.

Functionality, aesthetics, and ethics serve comfort, pleasure, and conscience respectively. Comfort is achieved by easier work: less physical or mental effort. Pleasure is achieved by clarity in expression. Conscience is served by limited use of resources. Simple artefacts serve one or more of these motives.

Figure 12
LifeStraw water filter
Design Vestergaard
Manuf. Vestergaard,
Switzerland
Simplicity for functionality. LifeStraw converts contaminated water into clean, safe drinking water. It makes life safer and simpler. Photo: INDEX: Design to Improve Life®

12

Apart from art and some fashion, most designed artefacts serve a practical function. However, the functional element can be more or less overshadowed by other considerations. The technical function of a bowtie is modest. In this case aesthetics matters more than functionality.

The table below codifies and exemplifies the seven possible combinations of the three motives for seeking simplicity. Some of the examples are debatable.

Simplicity motives			
Functionality ease of use	**Aesthetics** minimalism	**Ethics** austerity	Design examples
▒			Survival gear
	▒		Fashion
		▒	Religious artefacts
▒	▒		Sports gear
▒		▒	Basic vehicles
	▒	▒	Religious artefacts
▒	▒	▒	Shaker objects*
See The Shakers, p134			

13

Figure 13
Citroën 2CV, (1948) 1956
Design Flaminio Bertoni
Manuf. Citroën, France
Citroën 2CVs, VeloSolexes, and Danish Christiania load-bikes in their time all served a technical function while also – to varying degrees at different times in different places – connoting a message of leftism, solidarity or consumerism protest. Simplicity for functionality and ethics.

Figure 14
Canterbury Shaker Village, Canterbury, New Haven, CT, USA
Functionality, aesthetics, and ethics were all part of the Shakers' material culture.

14

Simplicity is not necessarily a result of one or more of the three stated motives: functionality, aesthetics, or ethics. Simplicity can also be the result of mental or material constraints. Primitive technology and limited resources are major causes of simple physical solutions to life's material problems. Just a few generations ago, our ancestors practised a simple life without intending to do so. Simplicity was determined by the lack of economic and technical development rather than choice. The same mechanism works in developing societies today.

During the Second World War, the UK introduced *utility furniture* and *utility clothing* to comply with rationing imposed by shortages of timber and textiles for purposes not directly related to the war effort.

In retrospect, or at a physical distance, we may appreciate the aesthetics of the simple rural life of past centuries, or in less developed parts of the world today. This does not mean that this life was, or is, the result of aesthetic considerations, or that those involved enjoyed, or enjoy, the aesthetic qualities that we appreciate from a safe distance in time or space.

There can be a world of difference between the ways in which we experience intended simplicity and forced simplicity. While simple surroundings can be a blessing to those who chose them, they can be a plague to those confined by them. Sometimes, however, ends meet. This happens when those forced into simplicity focus on the bright side of their situation: we don't have much. Let's accept the material limitations and focus on more important aspects of life.

Figure 15
Johannes Vermeer:
The Milkmaid, 1660 ca.
The simplicity of 17th century living was not the result of a choice, but a predicament dictated by lack of economic and technological development.

Figure 16
Null Stern Hotel, Zurich, Switzerland, 2008
Former prisons and nuclear bunkers that today function as successful holiday hotels exemplify the psychological difference between forced and intended simplicity. The Null Stern (Zero Star) Hotel in Zurich is located in a former nuclear bunker revamped by artists Frank & Patrik Riklin.

15

16

During the Second World War, the UK suffered from a shortage of timber for furniture production due to the U-boat menace, the rebuilding needs, and the war effort. At the same time, the demand for furniture increased because a high number of homes were destroyed by bombs. To cope with the gap between supply and demand, the UK prescribed a command economic measure involving special utility furniture, authorised furniture factories, and ration coupons reserved for newly married couples and blitz victims.

The government delegated the design of utility furniture using scarce resources in sensible ways to an Advisory Committee including Gordon Russell, well-known designer and furniture manufacturer. The committee presented its designs in the *Utility Furniture Catalogue* of 1943. The catalogue included five sections: living room, bedroom, kitchen, nursery furniture, and miscellaneous. The furniture was made of oak and mahogany. Furniture production that deviated from prescribed designs without permission could lead to imprisonment.

There were 700 furniture factories across the country authorised to manufacture utility furniture. The rationale behind the distributed net of manufacturers was to save transportation costs. In principle, no consumer should buy furniture from more than 15 miles away. Those eligible to buy utility furniture would fill in an application form from their local fuel office. If accepted, the applicant would receive a *Permit to Purchase*. Less fortunate furniture customers were referred to second-hand furniture, perhaps bought in the department stores that introduced new departments for pre-owned furniture.

The restrictions on the furniture trade continued after the war until 1952. New lines of utility furniture were introduced, but not successfully. The public wanted something more flamboyant and sometimes bought – illegally – decorated utility furniture on the black market. Forced simplicity has its limitations.

Figure 17–18
Pages from *Utility Furniture Catalogue*, UK, 1943
Sound in construction, agreeable in design, and reasonable in price were the sales arguments for utility furniture designed to save wood and other scarce resources.

INTRODUCTION

by the

Rt. Hon. Hugh Dalton, P.C., M.P.

President of the Board of Trade.

THIS booklet describes and illustrates the first edition of utility furniture. In extending utility production to this new field, my aim is to provide, for those who really need it, furniture which is sound in construction, agreeable in design and reasonable in price. Materials available for furniture-making are to-day very scarce, but, as these pages show, the designers have done their job well. Mr. Charles Tennyson, the Chairman of my Advisory Committee, and his colleagues, have devoted much time and many valuable ideas to this interesting new venture.

Hugh Dalton.

Page 1

17

LIVING ROOM

The living room furniture is in oak. The dining chairs have loose, padded seats covered with leather cloth, in a variety of colours.

SIDEBOARD : Second Section—Model 1a
Price £10.7.0

SIDEBOARD : Second Section—Model 1b
Price £10.7.0

Sideboard, with doors open, showing inside shelves. The sideboards are 4 ft. wide, 2 ft. 9 ins. high and 1 ft. 6 ins. deep.

DINING CHAIR:
Second Section—Model 3a
Price £1.9.0

DINING CHAIR:
Second Section—Model 3c
Price £1.9.0

Page 5

18

Ease of production – *Machbarkeit* in German – could have been listed as a motive for simplicity along with functionality, aesthetics, and ethics. However, ease of production is not an ultimate goal, but a way to reach the goal. Ease of production deals with means rather than ends.

Ease of production of a new product design is a function of the design and the available technology. What is impossible with one technology may be suitable for production with another technology. Considerations for ease of production work in two directions: designers design with a view to available technology and companies develop technology with a view to new designs. Ideally, these efforts go hand in hand. Sometimes the designer develops the new technology that enables production of his design.

Due to primitive technology, products of primitive societies are as often made simple by necessity as by choice. They are low tech and the simplicity is forced rather than wanted. Even then, the resulting products may have considerable functional and aesthetic value and may also have a life after the introduction of new technology. They may be wanted for their simple, 'honest', and understandable design. Industrialised countries import, or produce, and use numerous more or less generic products which were originally designed with a view to then existing limited technology, but which have proved to be so well suited for their purpose that they have survived technological development. Hat and basket weaving are examples of trades with minimal demands on technology, and trades where the products are not surpassed in quality by more advanced technology.

19

Figure 19
Geta, traditional Japanese footwear
Geta are wooden thong sandals elevated by plinths that also let the sandals serve as wellingtons. Geta are typically used together with a yukata or a kimono. When worn outdoor together with a kimono the elevation protects the kimono from being stained by mud. Geta come in many heights.
Geta make no distinction between left and right. Like other traditional tools geta were designed originally with a view to production with limited technology.

Figure 20
Orange Scissors, 1967
Design Olof Bäckström
Manuf. Fiskars, Finland
The Orange Scissors represent a happy marriage between ease of production and usability. To Fiskars the design means simplified production: the blades are cut out of a sheet of stainless steel. To the users the design with orange, ergonomically friendly ABS handles means a beautiful, well functioning hand tool.

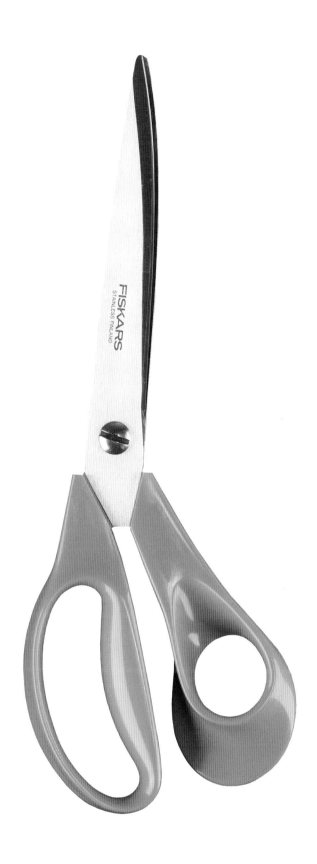

20

Sometimes a simplifying design cannot happen
before a new technology is introduced. Sometimes
this new technology is developed by the designer.
This happened in the case of the Viennese bentwood
chair. It epitomises the technology used, in fact the
whole idea of *Machbarkeit,* the intimate connection
between design and available technology.

Michael Thonet, the designer of Konsumstuhl Nr.14,
aka Coffee shop chair no.14, first invented a system
for layering wood to be bent for furniture. After
meeting problems with patenting his invention,
Thonet went on to bending wood in hot steam.
The steam bending technique enabled elegant and
strong chair design especially suited for use in public
spaces.

Michael Thonet designed Konsumstuhl Nr.14, the
world's first truly mass-produced chair, in 1859. The
construction enabled economical transportation
in parts to be assembled at the destination. It
prefigured later knock-down furniture, a hallmark
of IKEA. Konsumstuhl Nr.14 is one of the most sold
chairs in the world – in 1930 the sales exceeded 50
millions.

Simplifying design is far
from always waiting for
new technology. Sometimes
available technology is
waiting for a designer to
combine two existing
elements. Take wheeled
suitcases: inconceivable that
heavy luggage and small
wheels should wait so long
time before being introduced
to each other.

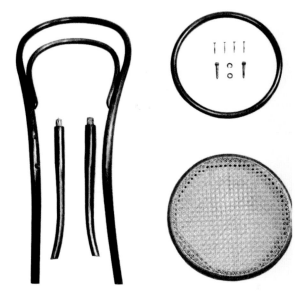

21

Figure 21–22
Coffee shop chair no.14, 1859
Design Michael Thonet
Manuf. 1859, Gebrüder
Thonet, Austria
Manuf. today: Thonet,
Germany

22

Although simplicity is a matter of subjectivity to a considerable degree, we can identify some general factors that may influence the simplicity of a tool, a building, a town, a system, a process, visual communications, or anything else. The degree to which a whole is conceived as being simple depends generally on three factors: number of elements, variety of elements, and structure. Number of elements influences quantity-simplicity and quality-simplicity. Variety of elements and structure influence quality-simplicity.

Number of elements. The number of parts or elements involved generally influences the simplicity of a whole. As a broad rule, more elements or parts mean less simplicity. However, a large number of elements in a whole does not necessarily compromise simplicity if the elements are more or less identical and systematically organised. In fact, repetition can have a calming effect. The distinction between the two simples is relevant here.

Variety of elements. The simplicity of a whole is generally influenced by the variety of the elements included. More variety in appearance can mean more or less simplicity. If variety in form is used to indicate variety in function and to guide operation, the variety in form may add to simplicity in use. A dashboard with all buttons identical may appear quite simple on a superficial level. However, the dashboard may be simpler to operate if the knobs for different functions have different forms. The diversity will facilitate 'reading' the buttons by seeing as well as by touching. If, on the other hand, variety in form is used as pure decoration, or just is the result of lacking planning, it may compromise the simplicity of both appearance and use.

Structure. The simplicity of a whole is generally influenced by the way the whole is structured, how comprehensibly the elements relate to each other. A comprehensible structure may depend on such factors as pattern, sequence, grouping, and procedural flow. Less logical structure means less simplicity.

Figure 23
Willys M38 Jeep, 1950
Manuf. Willys, USA

Figure 24
Concorde supersonic airliner, 1969
Manuf. Aerospatiale, France / British Aircraft Corporation, UK

Figure 23–24
More elements most often mean less simplicity. The greater the number of elements the more important become variety and structure. The cockpit's user interface in a Concorde supersonic aircraft was less simple than the dashboard of a Willys jeep, but functional spatial structure and variety of buttons assisted operation.

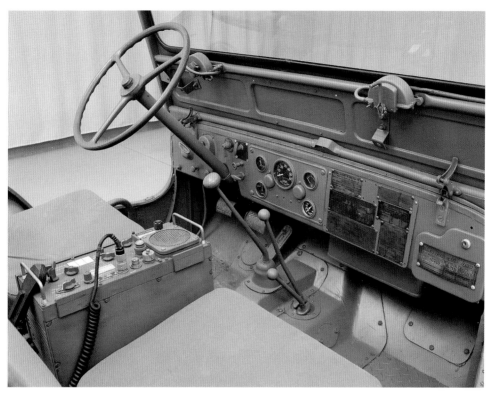

23

24

Dyson vacuum cleaners demonstrate that simplicity includes several different phenomena which concurrently can exist or happen on different levels. While Dyson vacuum cleaners appear more complex than most of their competitors they include technical features that mean a noteworthy simplification of the vacuum cleaning process. Dyson vacuum cleaners don't need bags but collect the dust in a see-through container, a feature which has been widely emulated by the competition.

Irritation concerning a malfunctioning vacuum cleaner, inspiration from a sawmill that removed sawdust by industrial cyclones, and endurance were three essential factors behind Dyson's success.

Dyson vacuum cleaners build on cyclone technology which, until James Dyson grabbed the idea, was used exclusively industrially. In Dyson vacuum cleaners the cyclone technology centrifuges the dust and other particles into a bin. A process that – much to the dismay of bagselling vaccum cleaner competitors – makes disposable bags redundant. Cordless models that recharge while not being used simplify the vacuum cleaning process further. As to the endurance, James Dyson, reportedly made 5,000-plus models of his vacuum cleaner before he was satisfied with the result. The company was established and the first Dyson vacuum cleaners were introduced on the UK market in 1993.

Why do Dyson vacuum cleaners have their multifaceted unsmooth surface? Two answers come to mind. The Dyson cleaners are new products, that later in their development will be smoothed, as it happened to cars, telephones, and scores of other products, consumer and industrial. Another possible answer is that James Dyson, the inventor and company owner, is an engineer who just wants to share the view of his invention.

Figure 25
Dyson DC59 Animal
Handstick Vacuum Cleaner,
2013
Design James Dyson
Manuf. Dyson, UK

25

In his book, *Emotional Design: Why we love (or hate) everyday things*, Donald A. Norman suggests that designed objects can be experienced in three different ways. He describes three types of design that facilitate these types of experience and call them visceral, behavioural, and reflective design.

Visceral experience stands for immediate experience, rather than use or consideration.

Behavioural experience stands for experience of the product's functionality based on use.

Reflective experience stands for experience based on close consideration.

Certain links exist between Norman's three kinds of design experience and the three motives for seeking simplicity: functionality, aesthetics, and ethics. The compliance of the kinds of design experience with each singular motive is exclusively, or primarily, felt in one singular kind of design experience.

Norman, Donald A.
Emotional Design: Why we love (or hate) everyday things
Basic Books, New York, 2005

Design experience related to simplicity motives			
Motive	Design experience		
	Visceral	Behavioural	Reflective
Functionality		x	
Aesthetics	x	(x)	(x)
Ethics			x

Functionality is experienced behaviourally, by use. What else?

Aesthetics is primarily enjoyed viscerally, by intuition, but also behaviourally, and reflectively, by use and by consideration.

Ethics is enjoyed by reflection, by consideration.

Figure 26
Ivory salt and pepper set, bought early 1970s
Design Schwartz
Manuf. Schwartz, Denmark
Visceral experience of the salt and pepper set involves the immediate appreciation of the material and craft.
Behavioural experience deals with the practical use. Is the pepper mill easy to operate?
Reflective experience involves thinking about the artefact, perhaps the ivory's provenance (this set was turned and acquired before the 1990 ban on international trade with ivory).

26

Beyond design

Simplicity is not confined to products and visual communications, or other design manifestations. Simplicity and the contrasting qualities of complexity and complication are found in any concept, body of thought, or intellectual work we can think about. British composer Benjamin Britten wrote a *Simple Symphony*.

This chapter of *Simplicity: A Matter of Design* addresses simplicity in a number of fields as diverse as science, microeconomics, user behaviour, business, and processes. However distant from design these fields may appear, they all by analogy shed light on simplicity in the design of products and communications.

Berthold Brecht
It is the simple things that are difficult to make.

Douglas Hofstadter
The idea of simplicity is a real can of worms, for what is simple in one vocabulary can be enormous complex in another vocabulary – and vice versa.

E. F. Schumacher
Any intelligent fool can make things bigger, more complex, and more violent. It takes a touch of genius – and a lot of courage – to move in the opposite direction.

Occam's Razor or *the law of parsimony* is a scientific principle attributed to William of Occam (1287–1347), an English logician and Franciscan friar. The principle that was given its name after William of Occam's death says: *Entities must not be multiplied beyond necessity.* This means that if two theories make the same predictions, the theory with fewest unproved assumptions – the simplest theory – should be preferred. Occam's Razor shaves off what is not needed.

Many great scientists have used, referred to, and discussed Occam's Razor. Sir Isaac Newton phrased his own version: *We are to admit no more causes of natural things than such as are both true and sufficient to explain their appearances.*

Later, Occam's Razor has been interpreted with considerable latitude. Some scientists use it to choose between theories with different predictions. Some use it to cut out features that cannot be observed. Some use it as a general call for simplicity in science and elsewhere.

A design-oriented interpretation of Occam's Razor would be something like

  eliminate superfluous elements.

In tools and visual communications that dictum addresses both functional elements and their visual presentation. Designers should dispense with unnecessary functional features and unnecessary form.

Figure 27
Poster for the Stockholm Exhibition, 1930, Sweden Design Sigurd Leverentz
The popular perception of the poster for the 1930 Stockholm Exhibition that introduced functionalism in Scandinavia shows how close the razor metaphor lies to popular design understanding. The poster intentionally presents a pair of wings inspired by an Egyptian birdman. However, lay Stockholmers saw no wings. They saw a razor that had shaved away all superfluities at the exhibition, and dubbed the symbol accordingly.

27

Economists use *the law of diminishing returns* to describe situations where businesses get lesser output per input unit the more input they allocate to a certain process. Marginal returns get smaller and smaller. Microeconomic theory says that businesses should stop the input when the value of the last unit of input equals – before it surpasses – the value of extra output. In small words: the businesses should continue the input only as long as it pays.

The law of diminishing returns is universal. It also works outside a strict business context. It is in fact reflected in many everyday activities. When we water our garden when it is parched after a hot summer day the first litres of water are extremely useful. If we, encouraged by positive feedback, go on and perhaps increase the amount of water it will have less and less positive effect. At some point, feedback will be negative. Finally the plants will drown.

In some situations, the marginal return can even become negative if input is not limited. Imagine a product that is advertised so much that the potential buyers get fed up with it, find it too common, lose interest, and buy less than before the product was advertised. There are situations where *any* additional input means a reduction in the output.

Standards are one absolute more-is-less category. The original purpose of standards is to coordinate. Standardised pictograms should facilitate fast communication by being immediately understandable to people across language and cultural barriers. One all-embracing standard is of course preferable to many competing standards. One reason that there are several pictogram standards and different pictograms with identical messages is that many sponsors consider pictograms a means of identification and branding rather than of assisting visitors finding their way. That is the reason why Olympic Games and World Expos introduce their own ranges of pictograms.

Figure 28
Three-, five-, and ten-sided polygons
The edgedness of regular, convex polygons constitutes an absolute more-is-less category. These Euclidean polygons become less edged – and more roundish – the more edges they have.

Figure 29–32
Examples of uncountable different standards for toilet pictograms

Figure 29
ISO toilet pictograms
The international standard is badly communicated to the public and sparsely used.

Figure 30
AIGA toilet pictograms
The copy free pictograms published by the Professional Association for Design are probably more used than the international standard.

Figure 31
Californian toilet pictograms
The Californian toilet signs were designed to allow blind people to feel the gender difference.

Figure 32
Expo 98 Lisbon toilet pictograms
Design Shigeo Fukuda

28

29

30

31

32

Everything used to be much simpler in bygone times when we had fewer choices, when simplicity was a predicament. In *The Paradox of Choice*, Barry Schwartz describes how the number of choices has grown beyond imagination while we would be better off with fewer choices in many situations. The abundance of choices is ubiquitous. It overwhelms us when shopping, when choosing clothes, car, education, pension scheme, and health care. Desirable freedom of choice tends to become a burden rather than a blessing, says Schwartz. The copious choices make us insecure before, while, and after we choose. How do we make the right choice? What are the missed opportunities? Shouldn't we have chosen something else? We can even regret our choice before we make it. More choices make us less happy. *Maximisers*, those who always go for the best, suffer more than *satisficers*, those who settle with enough.

Schwartz, Barry
*The Paradox of Choice:
Why More is Less*
Ecco, New York, 2004

In *The Long Tail* Chris Anderson suggests that it is not the number of choices that is the culprit, but the information provided. If the choices are presented in a well-structured way, many choices are preferable to few choices. Complexity in numbers is neutralised by simplicity in presentation. The future will bring more choices, assures Chris Anderson.

Anderson, Chris
*The Long Tail:
Why the Future of Business is
Selling Less of More*
Hyperion, New York, 2006

In *Zag: The #1 Strategy of High-Performance Brands*, Marty Neumeier presents five forms of what he calls *market clutter:*

Neumeier, Marty
*Zag: The #1 Strategy of
High-Performance Brands*
New Riders, Berkeley, CA,
2006

Product	Too many products and services
Feature	Too many features in each product
Advertising	Too many media messages
Message	Too many elements per message
Media	Too many competing channels

**Figure 33
Shoe store, street market,
Ueno, Tokyo, Japan**

33

There are two easily identifiable causes behind the
modern abundance of products and services. One
is that when our lives become more specialised we
also need more specialised tools, other products,
and services. This may be described as *demand-
pull.*

Business and industry are eager to fulfill whatever
new needs and wants may emerge. In fact they
overperform and serially deliver more varieties
than asked for to distinguish their products from
those of the competitors. This may be described as
supply-push.

The problem is not only that categories of goods
and services become larger. It is also that the
number of categories grows. While having
simplified our daily life in many ways, we have
used the resulting spare time and energy to
choose new things to be done. The result is clear:
in one way or another, our day is filled with jobs,
problems, and obligations that together make
our life quite complex. The rule seems to be this:
complexity expands so as to keep us busy. This
is a close relative of Parkinson's Law given by C.
Northcote Parkinson: *Work expands so as to fill the
time available for its completion.*

Whenever we get rid of old problems we tend to
invent new problems to fill the void. When not
in war we compensate with games and high-
risk sport. When we get rid of physical work,
we compensate with mountain biking, running,
and pumping iron in the fitness centre. When life
becomes simple, we tend to compensate with new
complexity. The modern choice concerns the mix of
simplicity and burdens.

Processes, courses of action aimed at reaching a certain goal, can be swift and easy – or long and cumbersome. They can be simple or complicated. Business leaders make themselves a name by cutting the red tape, introducing lean manufacturing and many other more or less fashionable procedures, which all boil down to simplification of process.

In the airport, frequent flyers enjoy special privileges with fast lanes and shorter check-in time. One of the big advantages of the now extinct Concorde service between Paris or London and New York was the almost eliminated immigration procedure in New York's JFK Airport.

Supermarkets introduce quick cashier lines for customers with few purchases. Pay-stations on motor roads and bridges have fast lanes for regulars.

Many homes reduce food processing time to a few minutes by replacing the cookbook's recipes with the microwave heating time stated on the package of ready-made food. Simplified processes often come at a price, economically and sensorially. Tea bags, Nespresso capsules, and ink cartridges for home printers and fountain pens exemplify.

Sometimes, processes just vanish. That happened when computers pensioned off lead typesetting and when digital photography made film buying, loading, and processing obsolete for most photographers.

Figure 34
Concorde supersonic airliner, 1969
Manuf. Aerospatiale, France / British Aircraft Corporation, UK
The Concorde supersonic aircraft simplified air travel. The short flying time inspired the airlines to shorten terminal operations. Unfortunately, the Concorde service excelled at the expense of heavy fuel consumption and pollution of the environment.

34

Fierce competition forces businesses to offer more and more. Business and product development often becomes synonymous with adding on. Supermarkets add more products and more services and stretch opening hours. Airlines do not limit themselves to moving passengers from here to there, but increasingly care about whatever services can be added, airborne or earthbound.

At some point in the development of companies adding more features to their products or services, some companies may feel tempted to go zag when competitors go zig and make difference by reduction introducing no-frills products or services at reduced prices. Supermarkets, furniture stores, airlines, hotel chains, and car manufacturers are among businesses that have chosen this path.

The flight attendant of a no-frills airline will charge the passengers some dollars for a cup of coffee, but the passengers cannot possibly drink coffee for the amount of money they save by flying budget, possibly from and to more distant airports with less service before and after take-off. Passengers paying their own ticket – and some companies as well – like the concept and the joy of saving while being transported. In Zurich, the Null Stern Hotel (literally the zero star hotel) has introduced a hotel concept that does not earn one star (see p26).

Shoppers in a no-frills supermarket may look in vain for a cosy sales environment with perfectly filled shelves and seductive product promotions. Many branded goods glitter by their absence; the supermarket has replaced them with generic brands or not-so-known private labels. Also, shoppers must be prepared to look for speciality products elsewhere. The product assortment is as a rule mainstream, and only that.

Figure 35
PAL (Portable Audio Laboratory) AM-FM radio, 2002
Design Henry Klos / Tom DeVesto
Manuf. Tivoli Audio, USA
Three buttons on a radio are enough for most of us most of the time.

Figure 36
Tata Nano, 2008
Manuf. Tata, India
The Tata Nano low-cost car has a body of aluminium and a 33 bhp two-cylinder petrol engine. Tata Nano weighs half a tonne and sells for 100,000 rupees ($2,100).

35

36

Functionality – Simplicity for comfort

Three motives drive our demand for simplicity
in design: functionality, aesthetics, and ethics.
Aesthetics and ethics are dealt with in following
chapters.

Functionality is the raison d'être of most design.
A product's functionality is its ability to serve its
practical purpose. Functionality is often seen in
contrast to aesthetics and ethics, but these are not
mutually exclusive qualities and not necessarily
conflicting qualities.

All artefacts with a practical purpose – most
designed objects – are tools. They help us to do
something that otherwise would have been less
simple, or impossible, to accomplish. Among tools,
hand tools are both the working class and the
aristocracy. These extensions of hand and arm are
generally made with a dominant view to practical
considerations. However, as previously mentioned,
this does not prevent us from appreciating the
aesthetic qualities of these tools.

Henry Ford
Too many screws
Comment to the first design of new carburator for
the model A

Johann Wolfgang von Goethe
*Everything is simpler than you think and at the same
time more complex than you imagine.*

Kawana Koichi
*Simplicity means the achievement of maximum
effect with minimum means.*

Functionality is the predominant motive for seeking simplicity. The functionality of any tool or appliance includes three levels, each of which can be more or less simple. These three levels are perceivable affordance, readability, and ease of use. They deal with identification, understanding, and operation respectively.

A tool's *perceivable affordance*, **is the way it signals what it can be used for. Is it a printer, a photocopier, or both?**

A tool's *readability*, **deals with the way the tool explains how it should be used. Is the correct use evident directly from the tool's design? Or does it need instructions written directly on the tool, or in separate user instructions? The simplest tools tell us without words how they should be used. User instructions are often repair design. Had the design been more readable, users wouldn't need separate instructions.**

Perceivable affordance and readability deal with the cognitive aspects of the product's functionality. They answer the *whats* **and the** *hows*.

Products sometimes achieve a simple appearance at the expense of perceivable affordance and readability. The product does not reveal its use, what it is for and how it should be dealt with. Closet doors without visible hinges and with no handles may appear extremely simple in terms of aesthetic appearance, but not in terms of first-time operation. In other words: the closet is quantity-simple, not quality-simple. Are they really doors or just panels? How do we open them? Once we have learned to touch the doors in a certain way, the system is also quality-simple in terms of operation. In some systems, for instance certain kinds of emergency equipment, such a lack of immediately perceivable affordance and readability is not acceptable. The equipment should facilitate use by anybody anytime without, or almost without, instruction. To other systems, immediate understanding may be less critical.

Ease of use deals with the physical operation of the tool. Can we use this tool skilfully almost immediately, or will it, like playing the violin, take years of study and practice for proficiency? Difficult physical operation often makes first-time users insecure. Is this the right tool? Am I turning the handle in the right direction? Did I misunderstand something?

The three-part perspective on functionality can be applied to a tool as a whole and to the parts of it. A car may be seen as a whole or as a number of distinct subsystems: steering, refilling gas, changing wheels, etc. Functionality relates to all subsystems and the levels of perceivable affordance, readability, and ease of use are relevant to all subsystems.

Cars generally look like cars. Perceivable affordance is seldom a problem for the car as a whole. The user interface, however, differs from make to make. Not all knobs, switches, buttons, handles, and levers advertise their purpose and mode of operation equally well. What is this button for? Clock? Radio? Cockpit light? Are these steel parts really the tools for changing wheels? How should they be used? Is it easy?

The same tool may be simple in some respects and complicated in others. A car may be easy to drive and extremely difficult to maintain and repair.

37

38

39

40

Figure 37–40
Citroën DS, 1955
Design Flaminio Bertoni
Manuf. Citroën, France
It is obvious that the new Citroën has fallen from the sky, said Roland Barthes, but is it a very simple or a very complicated car? That depends on the focus. In terms of appearance and driving, Citroën DS is a simple automobile. In terms of maintenance – save repair – it is less simple.

Simplicity can be conducive to good perceivable affordance, readability, and ease of use, properties that make products effective. However, the benefits of simplicity are not confined to effectiveness. Effectiveness is an absolute concept. Simplicity can also promote efficiency, a relative concept involving both effort and result. Efficiency is the ratio of output to input. We want elegant efficiency, small efforts leading to great results, simple solutions to complex and complicated problems.

Responsible inventors and designers strive to be ecologically sensible, making efficient use of scarce resources, another possible benefit of simplicity.

Mirrors applied with imagination are a case in point: small means used to achieve great results. Mirrors expand our vision dramatically. Without mirrors we can look forward and slightly sideways, but we cannot look backwards without turning. We are not born with rear vision. Also, we cannot see around corners or through solid masses. We need mirrors for such activities; they make our eyes mobile. With mirrors we can see ourselves, behind ourselves, and around corners. Periscopes with mirrors or prisms allow viewers to see without being seen. Mirrors are simple solutions with great effect: elegant simplicity. Luckily, our everyday is rich with elegant simplicity: zippers, bikes, Velcro, wheels on bags, etc.

Fighter jets, some commercial aircrafts, and some cars feature HUD, head-up displays, that project instrument readings on the windshield. This allows the pilots and drivers to keep their eyes ahead not interrupted by looking down on the instruments.

Figure 41
Periscope in US submarine, WWI
Periscope means *looking around*. Periscopes enable observation from concealed positions. They have most notably been used in submarines, tanks, and trenches. Simon Lake introduced the use of periscopes in submarines in 1902 while Sir Howard Grubb is credited for their perfection in WWI.

Figure 42
Periscope viewers at the Pantomime Theatre, Tivoli Gardens, Copenhagen
In the fifteenth century periscopes were used to see over the heads of crowds at religious festivals in Germany. Later, vertically challenged spectators in the Tivoli Gardens without a seat ticket hire periscopes to watch the performers' pantomimic gestures.

41

42

43

Figure 43
Hotel Reisen, Stockholm
Redesign 1960s
Stockholm's Hotel Reisen
occupies a rebuilt warehouse
at the Old City's waterfront.
Most of the guest rooms face
a narrow alley. To avoid the
otherwise dull views from
the guestrooms, the architect
prescribed mirrors mounted
on the inside of vertically
hinged shutters. Permanently
open at 45 degrees, the
shutters provide the guest
rooms with ample daylight as
well as delicate sea views.

44

45

46

Figure 44–46
HUDs, Head-up displays, are transparent displays that allow the user to get the necessary information without looking down on instruments. HUDs were first used in military aircraft but since then have been used in commercial aircraft, cars and motorcycle helmets. In aircrafts and cars the information is projected on the windshield. The information provided by car HUDs is typically speed and GPS navigation instructions. Peripheral HUD devices can be installed In any car.

Figure 44
BMW Head-up display
Manuf. BMW, Germany

Figure 45
BikeHUD
Manuf. Motorcycle
Information System
Technologies, UK

Figure 46
Garmin HUD for instalment
in any car.
Manuf. Garmin, USA

Simplicity can exist in several subfunctions of a product, each with respect to perceivable affordance, readability, and ease of use. A product can be simple on some levels in some subfunctions and not simple in others. Greater simplicity in one respect is often balanced by less simplicity in one or more other respects. This applies to levels as well as to subfunctions.

The trade off between simplicity in different respects is also seen in the production–distribution–use chain. One player's comfort may be paid by another player's discomfort. Simplicity is always seen from a certain vantage point. One-size-fits-all designs mean a simple solution to the supplier, but not necessarily to the user. It is no fun to wear wrong size clothes. One-size-fits-many is a more user-friendly concept, if we can't have one-size-fits-one.

Buyers of IKEA furniture may wonder why the cheap knock-down furniture has so many parts. The explanation is simple: to keep prices down, IKEA keeps transport and storage costs at an absolute minimum. To IKEA, simplicity in furniture design means furniture packed with as little volume as possible. To this end, the furniture is manufactured in small pieces. Hence IKEA's brown cardboard boxes are filled with furniture parts rather than with air. Simplicity in logistics, however, may reduce simplicity in assembly. It takes time to assemble the multitude of furniture parts. On the positive side, the use of small parts accommodates standardisation and use of the same type of part in several types of furniture.

The distribution of simplicity and complication between seller and buyer may work in both directions. Sometimes, the buyer reaps the fruits of simplicity made possible by some complication on the seller's side. One-stop shopping, the idea that the shopper can do all his shopping at one place, may be a convenient and simple arrangement for both shoppers and shop owners. Ideally, sellers and buyers share the advantages of scale.

Figure 47
**IKEA parcels with furniture
Manuf. IKEA, Sweden**
To IKEA simple means furniture packed in a flat cardboard box. To minimise transport and storage costs IKEA breaks furniture down into small parts. The smaller the parts, the larger the possibility for use in many different products.

47

Making products – tools – simpler can happen in several ways. The following approaches address one or more practical aspects such as production, appearance, perceivable affordance, readability, and ease of use. As already established, simplification in one respect will often mean complication in another. The often repeated adage *there is no such thing as a free lunch* applies here. Simplicity is typically a scarce quality that must be distributed from an overall view.

Reduction. The most obvious way to simplify designed products is to cut away something: to make things smaller, to remove superfluous material, elements, ornament, functions, or features, to cut to the bone. Design by subtraction. Reduction, however, is not a foolproof approach. Reduction should be used with care. It can both simplify and complicate elsewhere.

One simple way of reduction is scaled-down use of materials. This method will typically stress the need for material strength: less material without loss of strength. This can be done by stronger materials or intelligent use of materials. Eyewear of titanium thread and car bodies of corrugated iron exemplify these methods respectively. Intelligent use of corrugated iron and other materials is not a newcomer. Junkers aircraft, petrol cans, and roof plates of iron or asbestos all achieve strength by corrugation. Today, mineral water often comes in ultra-thin ribbed plastic bottles.

Figure 48
Air Titanium, 1987
Design Dissing+Weitling
Manuf. Lindberg Optik, Denmark
Simplicity by reduction.
Titanium frames celebrate the ultimate material economy. Weight 2.3 grams without lenses.

Figure 49
Junkers Ju52, 1932
Manuf. Junkers, Germany
Simplicity by reduction.
The corrugated duralumin fuselage combined strength with light weight.

Figurë 50
Citroën H, 1981
Design Flaminio Bertoni
Manuf. Citroën, France
Simplicity by reduction.
Like the 2CV Van, the Citroën H range produced 1947–1981 was an exercise in simplification. The corrugated body meant more strength with less material.

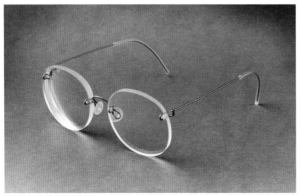

48

49

50

Specialisation. Division of a tool into two or more separate tools may clarify and strengthen separate functions by specialisation. A dedicated screw machine is simpler in use than a combined screw and drill machine. Spanners are simpler in design and simpler in use than adjustable wrenches – in some situations.

Professions and trades have always worked to increase their efficiency by specialised tools. Examples are legion. Patients notice the battery of tools dentists have at their disposal. Silversmiths working with hollowware have a large set of hammers each with a special function.

When it comes to specialised tools, sportspeople are at the fore. Pride and pure pleasure may fuel their aquisition of specialised tools. The anglers' collections of lures and flies point in this direction. That a large set of specialised tools can have an effect is circumstantially evidenced by the rules of golf: they limit the use of different clubs in a round to 14. The reason is not to reduce the caddie's work conditions.

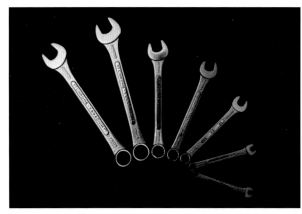

51

Figure 51
Open-end/ring spanners
Simplicity by specialisation.
In contrast to adjustable wrenches, spanners are the right tools when only foreseeable sizes of nuts and bolts must be dealt with.

Figure 52
Spread from *The Tool Book* by William Bryant Logan, 1997
Simplicity by specialisation.
You may call a spade a spade, but there is more to it: specialised spades for specialised spading.

Figure 53
Surgery tools
Simplicity by specialisation.
Surgeons (and dentists) use highly specialised tools for highly specialised jobs.

52

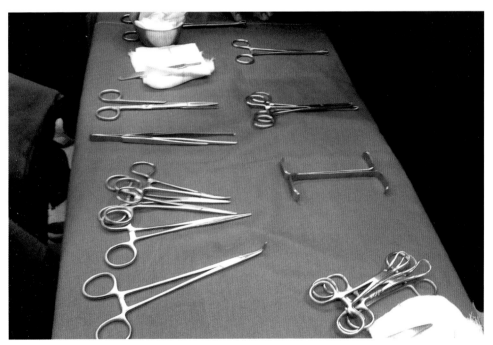

53

Modularisation. One obvious way to simplify complicated appliances is to compartmentalise the whole into a number of clearly separated, but still connected, units. Modularisation helps understanding the parts and the whole. Modularisation also facilitates detection of errors, and simplifies the repair and exchange of parts in case of malfunction. Replacement has more or less replaced repairs in modern cars. The garage does not repair a headlight; it replaces a well-defined part of the car.

Sometimes problematic parts of a tool or system are outsourced and treated as black boxes. A camera factory may leave the development and manufacture of lenses to another company. Car manufacturers leave the production of dozens of parts to subsuppliers. Aston Martins, Audis, BMWs, and Mercedes AMGs all feature Bang & Olufsen stereo sets.

In the bicycle industry the end products are more or less assemblies of outsourced components. Handlebars, saddles, derailleurs, gears, cranksets, pedals, wheels, and many other essential parts can be outsourced. Some cyclists compose and assemble their own vehicle.

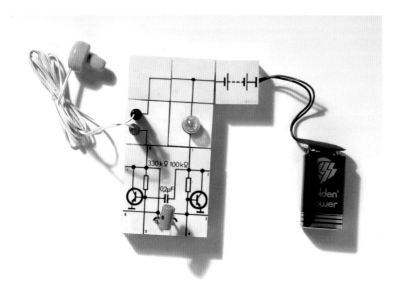

54

55

56

57

Figure 54
Braun Lectron, 1967
Design Dieter Rams /
Jürgen Greubel
Manuf. Braun, Germany
Modularisation as product
idea. Braun Lectron
electronic building blocks
compartmentalise the
technical functions in a
number of bricks that allow
numerous combinations and
facilitate learning.

Figure 55
SONY Cyber-shot DSC- W530.
JPG digital camera, 2012
Manuf. Sony, Japan
Simplicity by outsourcing.
Sony leaves the manufacture
of lenses for their Cyber-shot
cameras to Carl Zeiss. This
is simplicity in production
rather than in the finished
product.

Figure 56
B&O stereo set in Audi 8,
2014
Manuf. Bang & Olufsen,
Denmark
Simplicity by outsourcing.
Automotive manufacturers
traditionally outsource the
audio equipment.

Figure 57
Tokyobike 26, 2002
Design Ichiro Kanai
Manuf. Tokyobike, Japan
Simplicity by outsourcing.
Outsourced derailleur:
Shimano 8 speed with
Rapidfire shift lever.

Combination. Appliances with different functions that are used together or in similar situations can sometimes be combined to simplify the user's ownership and work. The Swiss army knife is the proverbial multitool, so much that it serves as a metaphor for anything with many abilities. Multitool complexity simplifies possession.

On a larger scale, the farmer's combine aggregates harvesting and treshing, two functions previously dealt with separately. The machinery has not become simpler. The operation has. At home, the lawnmower also collects the cut grass.

Mobile phones have made watches, calendars, calculators, and cameras redundant for many owners. Two separate functions, such as office printing and copying are combined in one implement that occupies less space and is cheaper than two separate machines. Combination and specialisation are opposite routes to simplicity. Danish physicist Niels Bohr comes to mind: *The opposite of a profound truth may well be another profound truth.*

Adjustable wrenches are simpler in use than one-size spanners – in some situations. An adjustable wrench is a continuous variable, it combines infinitely many tools.

59

58

Figure 58
Soldatenmesser 08, 2008
Manuf. Victorinox,
Switzerland.
Simplicity by combination.
Best known for the *Swiss army knife*, in Switzerland known as *Offiziersmesser*, Victorinox also makes the trank-and-file knife used in the Swiss army since 2009.

Figure 59
Adjustable wrench, 1991
Design Johan Petter Johansson (original model)
Manuf. Bahco, Sweden
Simplicity by combination.
An adjustable wrench is the appropriate tool when unforseeable sizes of nuts or bolts must be dealt with.

Figure 60
Ottakringer chair
Manuf. Section N, Austria
Simplicity by combination.
Chair-cum-ladder inspired by a 19th century chair found in a monastery in Tyrol.

Figure 61
70 series combine
Manuf. John Deere, USA
Simplicity by combination.
The combine takes care of harvesting and treshing in one operation.

60

61

Smoothing. Complicated contents can be united and simplified by a smooth surface. Many products start as crude assemblies of technical parts, but later get a smooth surface. Most modern appliances such as vacuum cleaners and other electric implements have smooth surfaces. Car designers also prioritise smooth surfaces, partly for aerodynamic, partly for aesthetic, reasons. They design the body early in the process and to some extent adjust intestines to fit the body. Modern cars often have more smoothing covers under the top cover. Under the hoods of BMWs, Audis, and Ferraris new picture-perfect surfaces meet the owner.

One decisive difference between scooters and motorbikes used to be the scooter's smooth surface. The designer of P46, the first Vespa scooter, Corradino D'Ascanio, allegedly hated motorbikes which he found bulky, dirty, and unreliable. In the patent application the manufacturer described P46 as

> *a motorcycle of a rational complexity of organs and elements combined with a frame with mudguards and a casing covering the whole mechanical part.*

Figure 62
Ducati 748, 1994
Manuf. Ducati Motor Holding, Italy
Simplicity by smoothing.
The fact that modern motor cycles are watercooled and don't need an air intake allows extensive fairings, shields that cover large parts of the machine room.

Figure 63–64
Simplicity by smoothing.
A scooter is a smoothed motorbike that protects the user from some unpleasant technical realities as well as wind.

Figure 63
Vespa P46, 1946
Design Corradino D'Ascanio
Manuf. Piaggio, Italy
It is interesting to notice how close this first scooter was to a generic solution.

Figure 64
Vespa 946, 2013
Manuf. Piaggio, Italy

62

63

64

Clarification. Internally complex appliances can have orderly user interfaces with great readability. The foreground covers, but represents, the background. Mechanical features located in different places under the car's hood may be brought together and be represented logically on the dashboard. The communications part of a product is essential to users, especially first-time users. Design history provides a proud list of companies that – in their time – prioritised products with clearly organised user interfaces: Olivetti, Braun, Bang & Olufsen, Sony, Apple.

To present complexity in a simple way, is the designer's noblest aspiration.

65

66

67

Figure 65
Exporter 2, 1954
Design hgf, Ulm Academy of
Design
Manuf. Braun, Germany
Simplicity by clarification.

Figure 66
Braun food processor, 1957
Design Gerd Alfred Müller
Manuf. Braun, Germany
Simplicity by clarification.

Figure 67
BeoSound 8, 2010
Design David Lewis
Manuf. Bang & Olufsen,
Denmark
Simplicity by clarification.

Figure 68
Olivetti Valentine, 1969
Design Ettore Sottsass with
Perry A. King
Manuf. Olivetti, Italy
Simplicity by clarification.
The handle makes it possible
to carry the typewriter with
one hand with or without its
case.

68

The principle of least effort was described by George Kingsley Zipf in 1949. However, the basic idea dealt with has been known as long as humans have jumped over where the hedge is lowest. The principle of least effort implies that we try to minimise our efforts – in the long run.

Being a linguist, Zipf described in great detail how the principle works in the way we use language. However, he suggested that the principle applies to all kinds of human work. Today, the principle is most often described as applied to, but is not limited to, information seeking in libraries. The principle suggests that given a choice of information sources information seekers tend to choose the easiest, not necessarily best, possibility.

Applied to seeking information about the use of technical implements, the principle of least effort will often mean choosing among a three-tier set of media: object, labels, user instructions. When we acquire a new electric tool, we don't read the user instructions if labels on the implement give the needed information. Further, we don't read the labels if the implement is self-explaining and we can immediately see how it should be operated. We prefer objects that are self-explaining. If they are not, we prefer to get along by reading labels: *on, off, forward, reverse*, etc. Finally, if absolutely necessary, we read the user instructions. We intuitively apply the principle of least effort. The three-tier set of information seeking styles involves increasing cognitive workloads:

Three-tier set of information media	
Information medium	Workload
Object	X
Labels	XX
User instructions	XXX

The principle of least effort is also part of the design process when designers instead of starting from scratch apply commercial off-the-shelf components.

Zipf, George Kingsley
Human Behavior and the Principle of Least Effort: an Introduction to Human Ecology
Hafner Pub. Co., New York, (1949) 1965

Figure 69
Sella stool, 1957
Design Achille Castiglione
Manuf. Zanotta, Italy
Sella is assembled of commercial off-the-shelf components, a practical instance of the principle of least effort.
Sella was designed at a time when telephones were typically wall hung. Sella offered the interlocutor a short time support.

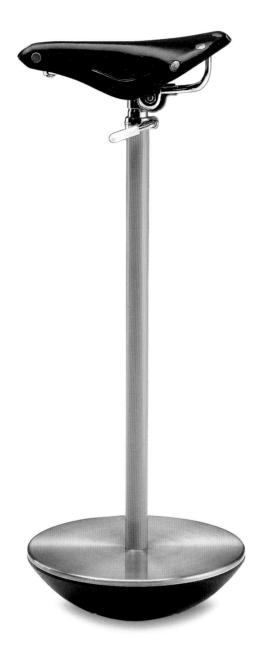

69

Probably, no company has as often as Apple been praised for simplicity. Apple's products, systems, outlets, communications, even Steve Job's product presentations, have been labelled *insanely* simple – to paraphrase Job's favourite qualifier.

While iPhone is the most sold Apple product so far, iPod, the portable media player, even more epitomises simplicity, in appearance, as in functionality. It combines a tangible media player with an intangible delivery system.

iPod was introduced in 2001 and has since then line-extended from iPod Classic into iPod Mini, iPod Nano, iPod Shuffle, and iPod Touch, each of which have developed into several generations. The *Classic* name was first introduced together with the sixth generation of the generic iPod, but is now also used about its ancestors. In 2007 100 million iPods had been sold.

The advanced electronics being concealed, iPod users experience at least three aspects of simplicity. One is the elegant appearance, another is the navigation, and a third aspect is the uploading of music, videos, and films.

The iPod is watchable, grabbable, and pocketable. *Menu, play/pause, next track*, and *previous track* are reached by 'buttons' in the click wheel. Scrolling through the menu and volume control are done by touching the click wheel in a rotational manner.

The click wheel in Classic, Nano, Mini, and Shuffle combines iconic appearance with fast navigation between 1,000 or more songs.

A considerable share of the iPod success must be attributed to iTunes Store, the online delivery system. iTunes Store is the world's largest music vendor with more than 37 million songs for sale.

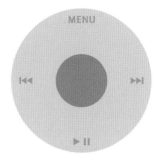

70

Figure 70
iPod click wheel, 2005
Design Synaptics
Manuf. Apple, USA
The click wheel was originally designed for iPod Mini, but has since then been used in all iPods apart from iPod Touch.

Figure 71
iPod Classic, 2006
Design Jonathan Ive
Manuf. Apple, USA

Figure 72
iPod Shuffle, 2005
Design Jonathan Ive
Manuf. Apple, USA

Figure 71–72
iPod is a product family with an expanding number of members.

71

72

However great our wish for simplicity, we do want some complexity. In fact we find some complexity necessary. A road bicycle racer needs several gears to adjust to changes in road gradient and wind conditions. The gear gives the bicycle the *requisite complexity* that lets the rider homogenise his movements by changing the distance that the bicycle advances per pedal stroke.

The requisite complexity concept is not a carte blanche to add any complexity that comes to the designer's mind. Requisite complexity expresses the needs that result from weighing the pros and the cons of more complexity. What does the user really need? What price must be paid? Can one design serve all users, or should some users have special models? Is mass customisation perhaps the solution that combines low unit costs with variety in offerings?

Requisite complexity can be undisclosed to the user. Designers choose between showing off complex technique and hiding background complexity behind the simplest possible foreground. In the case of bicycle gears the choice is between internal (real) gears and derailleur 'gears'.

Figure 73
14 speed hub gear, 1985
Manuf. Rohloff, Germany
Ordinary cyclists typically prefer internal gears, where complexity is hidden behind a smooth surface.

Figure 74
Shimano xt rear derailleur, 1985
Manuf. Shimano, Japan
Racing cyclists always use external gears. To be precise, external gears are not real gears since cogs do not mesh with one another, but drive, or are driven by a chain.

73

74

Manufacturers of many types of electronic appliances compete on functional features. When developing a mobile phone or other appliances, they are tempted to include as many technical features as possible. The result is that we all possess appliances that are grossly overqualified for our needs. These appliances irritate us. The problem is not so much that we have paid for something we do not need. The problem is more that these products steal our time and stress us. They are too complicated to use. More functions often mean less functionality. An example at hand is the Microsoft Word software used to write the manuscript for this book.

Manufacturers know that not all customers will need all functions, but by including as many functions as possible they aim to reach as many customers as possible. Of course, it is possible that some customers want as many functions as possible, for reasons of their own.

When companies try to pare down the number of product features, they typically do so for one of two – occasionally combined – reasons. One reason is to offer their products at a competitive price. This was described in the 'No frills' section (see p50). Another reason is to offer an alternative product to feature sceptics who just want to have the essential function – and sometimes are prepared to pay extra for the omission of not wanted features. In fashion, furniture, and architecture simplicity often comes at a price. That is a paradox.

Functionality
The paradox of simplicity

All bills must be paid; simplicity has a price. Sometimes the obvious simple design solution happens to be a very difficult solution that must be paid for with hard work, expensive materials, or complex processes – everything behind the curtain.

Building a Chesterfield chair by spraying liquid polyurethane from a hose and letting it stiffen layer upon layer was the simple idea of Danish artist and designer Gunnar Aagaard Andersen. When the first chair was built, the manufacturer told Aagaard Andersen that $400 worth of material had been used, a fortune in the 1960s. Aagaard Andersen's reply was simple: *Then we must find a more complex method.*

Devoted minimalist designers go far to create the attractive simplicity. They urge suppliers to deliver materials of extraordinary specifications and craftsmen to do jobs never tried before. Minimalist architect John Pawson specified floorboards that ran the full length of his London townhouse, a perfectly simple solution. The problem was that floorboards normally don't come in such lengths. The supplier finally sourced the floorboards from Denmark.

Figure 75–76
Polyurethane chair, 1965
Design Gunnar Aagaard Andersen, Denmark
Artist and designer Gunnar Aagaard Andersen in the act of building a Chesterfield-type chair of liquid polyurethane. Unfortunately, the price of material could not compete with that of traditional – more complex – techniques.

75

76

Several kinds of electronic communication and entertainment devices follow two apparently contradictory trends. They get more functions, and they become smaller. While there seems to be no lower limit for the size of electronics, the user interface must have a certain size to accommodate the human eyes and fingers. One apparent solution is to structure the control in a number of hierarchical layers, much like the way we know from phone trees, automated telephone information systems that speak to the caller with a combination of fixed-voice menus.

One device has ten different functions each addressed by one of ten dedicated buttons. That is a broad (shallow) solution. Another device has ten different functions, all addressed by one multifunction button that can be operated in ten hierarchical layers. That is a deep solution. Which device has the simplest visual appearance? Which device is simplest to operate?

Broad solutions involve operation in space. Deep solutions involve operation in time.

Deep solutions have come to stay. The surface of a mobile phone with scores of functions cannot contain scores of dedicated controls in a user-friendly size. The surface is not big enough. Most of the controls must be hidden backstage and only be summoned to the foreground when needed.

Introduction of multifunction controls for deep solutions can cause problems to the user. Not all buyers of BMW cars were enthusiastic when BMW introduced the iDrive system in their flagships. Manipulating the iDrive silver knob located in a console between the front seats, the driver has access to more than 700 functions dealing with driving, security, comfort, and entertainment. What was meant to be a simplification was – in the beginning – by many users experienced as a complication. Deep solutions tend to have less steep learning curves than broad solutions. They take longer time to learn.

Figure 77
BMW ConnectedDrive, New generation navigation system iDrive Touch, 2012
Manuf. BMW, Germany
BMW's iDrive system was first used in 2001 for the 7-series. It has since been developed into many other versions. Deep information structure.

Multifunction controls and deep solutions may take time to learn and to use. Special simplicity (see p20) is an advantage of scale that beginners cannot reap. The crucial question concerns which functions need dedicated controls – broad solution – and which functions can do with a multifunction control – deep solution. BMW cars with iDrive have dedicated controls for no-patience functions such as screen wiper, temperature, and sound volume.

77

User-centred design is not a new idea. The first design ever made was user-centred: the designer designed a tool for himself. The new thing is that designers who are in many respects remote from the end user take an increased interest in the end user's situation. What is the end user's real need? How will he read, understand, and react? How long will his learning curve be?

In their quest for simplicity, designers should always take the user's situation as their point of departure. What are the user's background and skills? How is the context of use? How important is fast understanding of the product? How should simplicity in appearance be weighed against simplicity in use. How should simplicity in first time use be weighed against simplicity in later use (general vs. special simplicity)?

Simplicity is subjective to a considerable degree. Simple audio equipment is audio equipment that is considered simple by its intended users. But different users have different backgrounds, different experiences, and different competencies. What is child's play to a hardcore hi-fi nerd may be absolutely intimidating to a technophobe.

Heterogeneous user groups can be dealt with as such or broken down to smaller, homogeneous subgroups. In the former case, the designer will seek solutions that almost all can use. This is inclusive design. In the latter case, the designer will design different solutions for user groups with different needs. This is exclusive design.

In many situations the designer can't have an informed idea about the capabilities of the possible users. That is for instance the case in design of much emergency equipment. Then the designer will look for a low common denominator. Simplicity over complication.

Figure 78
Viking RescYou Pro life raft for the yachting sector, 2013 Manuf. Viking, Denmark
Abandoning a yacht at sea in an emergency situation doesn't leave time for longer learning curves. The Viking life raft is designed with that in mind. All the sailors need to do is to get the raft out of its container, throw it into the water, and pull a string. General simplicity.
If the shipwrecked sailors have found time to study the instruction book they will know that they should preferably abandon the yacht from the lee side. They will also know how to repair the raft at sea should anything happen to it and many other things that will make life aboard the raft easier. These are the benefits of special simplicity.

78

That a tool is simple in terms of use means that
it is easy in terms of perceivable affordance,
readability, and operation. For tools that are not
used permanently in one location, but in isolated
periods and/or in different locations, storage
and transportation may be essential parts of the
operation. Both storage and transport may be
simplified if the tool is collapsible. The simplification
of storage and transport is achieved by complexity in
construction. In terms of construction, a folding knife
is more complex than a knife with a fixed blade.

In nature, collapsibility is a survival principle. Both
animals and plants adapt to changing circumstances
by reduction and expansion. Animals downsize to
hide, relax, rest, and protect themselves and upsize
to brag, threaten, fly, fight, and court. Flowers open
to attract pollinating insects and close to minimise
evaporation, maintain a more stable temperature, or
temporarily retain an insect to ensure the transfer of
pollen.

Two conditions must be met before human-made
collapsibles are conceived and created:

First, somebody must see an advantage in reducing
the volume a tool occupies when not in use.

Second, it must be mechanically possible to reduce
the volume of that tool or rather to redistribute the
volume. A newspaper or a tent does not become
smaller when folded. Their volumes are merely
distributed into formats that are more practical for
storage and transportation. *Collapsibles: An Album
of Space-Saving Objects* codifies twelve categories
of collapsibility: stress, folding, creasing, bellows,
assembling, hinging, rolling, sliding, nesting,
inflation, fanning, and concertina.

Collapsibility is a principle used in all kinds of
design, from the smallest pocketable objects, to
ladders, cranes, bridges, and shelters. Medécins Sans
Frontières use inflatable hospitals in emergency
areas.

79

Per Mollerup
*Collapsibles: A Design Album
of Space-Saving Objects*
Thames & Hudson, London,
2002

Figure 79
Opinel folding knife, 1890
Design Joseph Opinel
Manuf. Opinel, France
Even the simplest folding
knife is in terms of
construction more complex
than a knife with a fixed
blade.
Hinging is one of the most
common collapsibility
principles.

Figure 80
Stacking stools, 1932–33
Design Alvar Aalto
Manuf. Artek, Finland
Stacking is a principle of
collective collapsibility.

Figure 81
Calla funnel, 1997
Design Thomas Dickson
**Manuf. 1997, Royal
Scandinavia, Denmark
Manuf. 2004, Normann
Copenhagen, Denmark**
Bellows is the term of the
collapsibility principle used.

Figure 82
**Medécins Sans Frontières
inflatable hospital at
Bethany Hospital,
Tacloban, Philippines**
Inflation is the collapsibility
principle used.

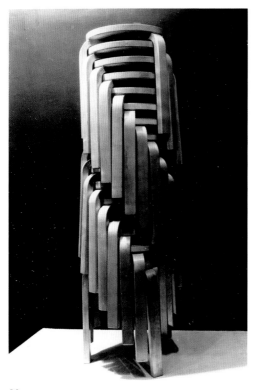

80

81

82

Aesthetics – Simplicity for pleasure

While functionality may be considered the heaviest
motive for seeking simplicity in design, the aesthetic
appearance is often the factor that immediately
signals the presence of simplicity.

Simplicity in design may please the eye of the
beholder in more than one way. We explore some of
them here. Although highly subjective, aesthetics
involves several guiding principles, some of which
may seem mutually contradictory.

Aesthetically attractive simplicity, occasionally does
more than please; it may advertise restraint by its
example and – by advocating simplicity – contribute
to husbanding scarce resources. This creates a
natural transition to the discussion of ethics that
follows in the next chapter.

Frédéric Chopin
*Simplicity is the final achievement. After one has
played a vast quantity of notes and more notes, it is
simplicity that emerges as the crowning reward of
art.*

Ludwig Mies van der Rohe (and others)
Less is more.

Stendhal
Only great minds can afford a simple style.

Diana Vreeland
Elegance is refusal.

Frank Lloyd Wright
The architect should strive continually to simplify.

Frank Lloyd Wright
*Simplicity and repose are the qualities that measure
the true value of any work of art.*

Minimalism or *minimal art*, is a label attached to the work of several American artists in the 1950s, 1960s, and 1970s, notably Donald Judd, Dan Flavin, Sol Lewitt, Carl Andre, and Robert Morris. These artists did not create the label; an art critic did. Nor did they write a manifesto or consider themselves to be a formal group.

83

The limited number of effects used by these artists justify the term *minimal art*. The artists tried to free their works from personal expression, to allow the spectator greater freedom of experience. The aim was to free spectators from being distracted by composition and theme. Industrial materials, monochromatics, repetition, and the absence of organic lines characterise most minimal art.

The minimalists made no secret of taking inspiration from architecture. Later, architects and architecture critics appropriated the term *minimalism*. Now the term was used about aesthetically simple buildings and other simple objects with utilitarian purposes. The characteristics are primarily absence of ornament, clear structure, repetition, and limited variety. Ludwig Mies van der Rohe and other architects who reportedly inspired the minimalist artists were now, in turn, referred to as *minimalists*.

Today, the term *minimalism* is widely used in relation to architecture and design characterised by great visual simplicity. Aesthetics is the motive in play. Architects Tadao Ando, David Chipperfield, John Pawson, and Peter Zumthor are frequently referred to as minimalists.

Figure 83
Concreta, the Billy Rose
Art Garden, Israel Museum,
Jerusalem, Israel, 1988/1991
Design Donald Judd

Figure 84
Farnsworth House, Plano, IL,
USA, 1951
Design Ludwig Mies van der
Rohe
Mies van der Rohe and cohorts reportedly inspired the minimalist artists and were later themselves referred to as *minimalists*.

Figure 85
Therme Vals, Switzerland,
1993/1996
Design Peter Zumthor
Peter Zumthor's architecture carries all the hallmarks of minimalism.

84

85

While previous periods found it natural to embellish surfaces of buildings and utensils with decoration, modern designers and architects have expelled ornament to a considerable degree. The shape of the building or utensil should itself deliver the aesthetic experience. However, this dogma was not generally accepted overnight.

No one person is responsible for the death of the ornament, but Adolf Loos, the Austrian architect and critic, blazed the trail. Loos was a fervent opponent of ornament on objects with a utilitarian purpose and aired his views in speech and writing, famously in his essay *Ornament und Verbrechen*, Ornament and Crime, published in 1908.

Although Loos's farewell-to-ornament argument was economical in nature, his acolytes probably followed his dictum for aesthetic reasons. The buildings and interiors that Loos himself designed offered no pecuniary savings. Rich materials made up for the lack of human-made ornament, both informing the buildings and making them expensive. The Goldman and Salatsch edifice, Manz booksellers, and Knize gentlemen's outfitters shops, all in Vienna, serve as evidence.

Le Corbusier and other modernist architects had no problems with the ornament expelled. They compensated with monumental free art whenever they felt like. Also, both Le Corbusier and Mies van der Rohe freely entered the grey zone between pure ornament and structure. They adorned their buildings with structural elements not dictated by strictly constructive considerations.

I have discovered the following truth and presented it to the world: Cultural evolution is synonymous with the removal of ornament from articles in daily use.

Ornament is wasted manpower and therefore wasted health. It has always been that way. But today it also means wasted material, and both mean wasted capital.

Adolf Loos in *Ornament und Verbrechen*, Ornament and Crime, 1908

Figure 86
Goldman & Salatsch
Building, Vienna, 1910
Design Adolf Loos
In 'Looshaus' as in other Loos buildings rich materials fully make up for the lack of human-made ornament.

Figure 87
Haus Steiner, Vienna, 1910
Design Adolf Loos

86

87

88

Figure 88
Braun RT 20 Tischsuper,
pear wood / graphite, 1961
Design Dieter Rams
Manuf. Braun, Germany
The author's first radio,
bought with a considerable
discount due to lack of
demand.

Figure 89
Fireplace 2, 1970s
Design Nils Fagerholt
Manuf. Cubus, Denmark
Bellow and log grabber,
1972/1973
Manuf. Cubus, Denmark
Design Knud Holscher
Wall hung Fireplace 2
takes ancient heating into
contemporary living space
and functions both as an
open fireplace and as a
closed stove. The former
option favours vision, the
latter option favours heating.

89

Dieter Rams is primarily known for his design of audio and household appliances for Braun, but also for his furniture for Vitsoe, both of Germany.

Rams worked for Braun 1955–1995, first as interior architect and designer, later as head of the design department. During these four decades Rams changed our idea about what household electronics and audio equipment can look like.

Rams crystallised his design philosophy in phrases like *die leise Ordnung der Dinge*, the silent order of things. Order and simplicity are key to Dieter Rams's design. With his talent for organising surface, Rams domesticated audio and household appliances and gave complexity a simple face. Rams reduced the number of buttons and organised the remaining buttons in silent order. He restricted the colours for audio equipment to a grey scale while limiting the use of chromatic colours to special buttons.

Rams was ahead of his own time. Nicknames given to his designs serve as circumstantial evidence. The famous SK 4 Phonosuper with the see-through lid designed in partnership with Hans Gugelot from hochschule für gestaltung in Ulm became *the Snow White Coffin* and his white audio equipment was referred to as *kitchen appliances.*

Dieter Rams defined eleven principles for good design:

1 Good design is innovative
2 Good design makes a product useful
3 Good design is aesthetic
4 Good design helps us to understand a product
5 Good design is unobtrusive
6 Good design is honest
7 Good design is durable
8 Good design is consequent to the last detail
9 Good design is concerned with the environment
10 Good design is as little design as possible
11 Back to purity, back to simplicity

Figure 90
Braun Phonosuper, SK 4/ SK 5/SK 55, 1956
Design Dieter Rams / Hans Gugelot
Manuf. Braun, Germany
This radio grammophone –popularly referred to as *the Snow White Coffin* – was ahead of its time.

Figure 91
Vitsoe 606 Universal shelving system, 1960
Design Dieter Rams
Manuf. 1960, Vitsoe, Germany
Manuf. 2010, Vitsoe, UK
Among the furniture that Rams designed for Vitsoe, the shelving system stands out. It will remain longer on the market than any of the electronic products, which technological development will make obsolete.
A complex mounting system enables the simple appearance of the shelving system. However, once the system is mounted, the silent order will be enjoyed for decades.

90

91

Unconcealed structure was the great idea of
functionalist design and architecture. Following the
death of ornament, structure took over the role as
mâitre de plaisir. Simplicity and honesty were key to
good architecture. Unconcealed structure celebrating
the constructive principle became the major source
of aesthetic experience. The division between
supporting and supported elements delivered much
of the aesthetic argument in buildings designed by
Mies van der Rohe and cohorts. Since then, trend
setting architects have to a considerable degree sent
functional expression to the background considering
themselves to be free artists.

In furniture design, unconcealed structure still
counts as respected aesthetic currency. Furniture by
Charles & Ray Eames and by Poul Kjærholm blazed
the trail.

Figure 92
Seagram Building, New York,
1958
Design Ludwig Mies van der
Rohe / Philip Johnson

Figure 93
DWC, plywood dining chair,
1945
Design Charles & Ray Eames
Manuf. Vitra, Germany
In furniture design,
unconcealed structure still
counts as respected aesthetic
currency.
Eames's plywood chairs are
an example of design which
was made possible by the
designer's invention of new
technology, here for bending
plywood sheets in two
directions.

92

93

94

95

Figure 94
PK33 Stool, 1957
Design Poul Kjærholm
Manuf. 1957, E. Kold
Christensen, Denmark
Manuf. 2010, Fritz Hansen,
Denmark

Figure 95
PK80 Sofa, 1957
Design Poul Kjærholm
Manuf. 1957, E. Kold
Christensen, Denmark
Manuf. 2010, Fritz Hansen,
Denmark

Figure 96
DCM Dining Chair Metal,
1945-46
Design Charles & Ray Eames
Manuf. Herman Miller, USA

Figure 97
Skagen chair, 1985
Design Jørgen Gammelgaard
Manuf. 1985, Børge Schiang,
Denmark
Manuf. 2010, Bruno Hansen,
Denmark

96

97

In designing appliances with complex technical content, development has since long gone in the opposite direction of furniture design's unconcealed structure. The technology works undercover. Flashing sleek surfaces, smoothing, has been a favourite theme while the technical content is considered intestines (see p72).

98

In the 1930s Raymond Loewy and other American industrial designers made themselves a name by wrapping up technical insides in more or less streamlined outsides. In terms of visual appearance, Loewy's steam engine for Pennsylvania Railroad in 1939 meant a considerable simplification compared with its rail-borne forefathers.

Automobiles are interesting cases of outside simplification. The outside doubles as aesthetic pleaser and aerodynamic reducer. Both parts of this double function are of paramount importance.

When first invented, technical products typically look like assemblies of components, while later versions are hidden behind smoothing surfaces.

The early Danish designer Knud V. Engelhardt (1882–1931) made the observation that sharp edges on tools eventually would be rounded off during use. Engelhardt suggested that the designer right from the beginning should round off these edges to make the tools more user friendly. There is a curious parallel between this small-scale adjustment and the surface smoothing of larger artefacts such as household appliances, vehicles, and heavy machinery where contact in use includes other factors than the human body, for instance air and water. Smooth surfaces may also be an issue of workplace safety. Easing the physical contact with the artefact's surrounding and pleasing the eye may be parallel effects.

In some cases designers and manufacturers stick to impressive technical surfaces – perhaps in order to advertise the advanced technology.

Figure 98
Pennsylvania Railroad steam engine PRR S1, USA, 1939
Design Raymond Loewy
Early undercover technique.

Figure 99
Buick Y-job, 1938
Design Harley J. Earl
Manuf. General Motors, USA
The industry's first concept car complete with hidden headlamps, gunsight hood ornament, and waterfall grille.

Figure 100
Beolit 39, 1939
Manuf. Bang & Olufsen, Denmark
First Bang & Olufsen radio with bakelite cabinet. Bang & Olufsen reportedly took their inspiration for Beolit 39 from Harley J. Earl's Buick Y-job.

99

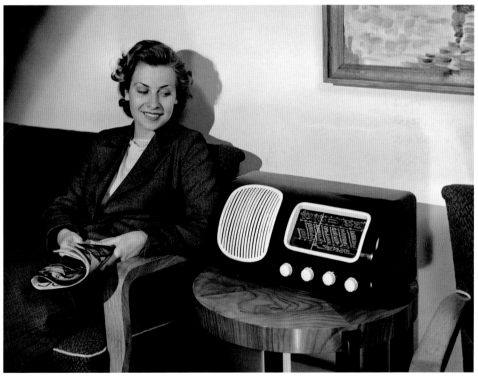

100

That some types of equipment are designed with purely functional considerations and that they appear strikingly simple do in no way prevent users from adoring and acquiring them for partly or exclusively aesthetic reasons. Clothing and accessories provide ample examples.

The nature of fashion is change, and changes will necessarily now and again take clothing items into something less functional. Shoes get more pointed, get higher heels, and offer less protection than the archetype. While this eclipse of reason lets many oddities appear some clothing items and accessories survive in their original, basic form partly on their functional merits partly on their seducing simplicity. Blue jeans, pea jackets, sweatshirts, deck shoes, aviator frames, and pilot's and diver's watches populate this intrepid chic category.

None of these functional turned fashionable products do better than the T-shirt illustrate the principle. Originally introduced as a piece of underwear in the American and English armies in the 1910s the T-shirt worked its own way out in the daylight supported by men in war as well as actors such as Marlon Brando, James Dean, and Paul Newman. That the T-shirt's white surface doubles as canvas for graphic messages has not obstructed its success. Several other products with cult status have a martial background.

Figure 101
Die grosse Fliegeruhr, the Big Pilot's Watch, 1940–2007
Manuf. IWC, Switzerland
Aviator watches used to be worn by pilots. *Die grosse Fliegeruhr* from IWC International Watch Company was official Luftwaffe watch during WWII. The watch is characterised by its considerable size, diameter 55 mm, and its robust winding crown that facilitates operation by a gloved hand. The extra-long wrist strap with double bow and clasp clip makes it possible to wear the watch over flight overalls.

Figure 102
Pilot's Watch Mark XVI, 2007
Manuf. IWC, Switzerland
Mark XVI epitomises the down to earth features of a good aviator watch. The omission of '3', '6', '9', and '12' on the dial hardly harms fast reading. Other aviator watches appear more sleek, more business class, less cockpit.

Figure 103
Staff wearing T-shirts in US Army emergency room, Korea, 1951

101

102

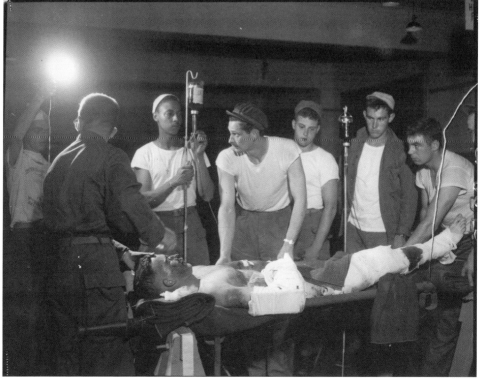

103

Brazilian composer Antonio Carlos Jobim did not
as advertised in the title of his *One note samba*. He
did not create a samba consisting of one note, but
surely fancied the idea. Designers harbour similar
aspirations and strive to design products comprising
as few parts as possible. When redesigning existing
products designers proudly announce the reduction
of the number of parts. The designers argue that
their reductive exercise cuts manufacturing costs,
and sometimes it does. The designers' ultimate
ambition is to make a product out of one piece of
material, to knit the sweater out of one thread.

A few generations ago, people living in rural areas
made and used all kinds of wooden one-piece
utensils: cube chairs, ladders, hooks, spoons, dishes,
bowls, walking sticks, and clogs. However old the
idea, it still has some merit, as demonstrated by
Apple's MacBook Pro machined from a single piece
of aluminium (see p113). According to Jonathan Ive
the unibody design means a thinner, lighter, and
more robust machine. Also, the Leica T camera is
carved out of one block of aluminium.

104

105

Figure 104
Tea whisk made of one piece
of bamboo, Japan

Figure 105
Traditional European clogs of
poplar wood

Figure 106
Vivianna watch, 1959
Design Torun Bülow-Hübe
Manuf. Georg Jensen,
Denmark
Watch and jewellery in one
piece.

Figure 107
Ole, 1997
Design Ole Jensen
Manuf. Royal Scandinavia,
Denmark
For more than 200 years,
designers and manufacturers
of drinking cups have added
an alien ear to the vessel.
Danish designer Ole Jensen
thought otherwise and
expanded the body into a
handle.

Figure 108
Ghost Chair, 1967
Design Cini Boeri /
Tomu Katayanagi
Manuf. Fiam Italia, Italy

106

107

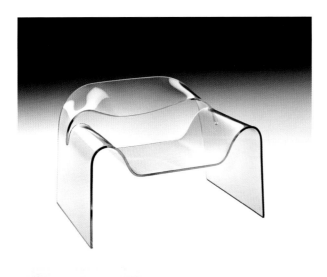

108

109

110

Figure 109
Panton chair, 1959/60
Design Verner Panton
Manuf. Vitra, Germany
Several furniture designers
have designed one-piece
furniture, but none more
elegantly than Verner Panton
who created the world's first
one-piece chair of plastic.

Figure 110
NXT Chair, 1991/1996
Design Peter Karpf
Manuf. Iform, Sweden

Figure 111
NON chair, 2002
Design Komplot
Manuf. Källemo, Sweden
NON is cast in one piece of
rubber (around a steel frame).

111

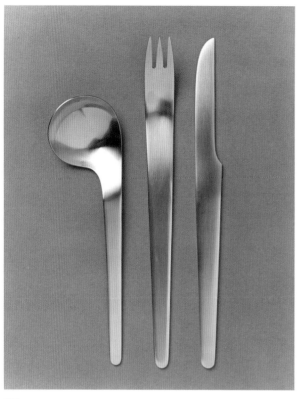

112

113

Figure 112–113
Several designers of flatware made knife, fork, and spoon each out of one piece of material. AJ and Blue Shark cutlery stand out with their simple, yet exciting, shapes.

Figure 112
AJ flatware, 1957
Design Arne Jacobsen
Manuf. Georg Jensen,
Denmark

Figure 113
Blue Shark flatware, 1966
Design Svend Siune
Manuf. Georg Jensen,
Denmark

Figure 114
MacBook Pro, 2008
Design Jonathan Ive
Manuf. Apple, USA
The case of MacBook Pro is made of a single block of aluminium. Apple used the oneness as a sales proposition: *MacBook Pro Unibody.*

Figure 115
Leica T, 2014
Design Leica / Audi
Manuf. Leica, Germany
When celebrating their 100 year anniversary with a new camera series, Leica teamed up with Audi's design group. Leica T resides in the first camera house in the world hewn out of one block of aluminium. Simplicity in appearance. By WiFi Leica T sends the pictures to the photographer's computer. Simplicity in use.

114

115

Repetition has a bad reputation. Repetition, the
opposite of variation, is stereotyped as the mother
of boredom. But there is more to it. Repetition in
architecture and design can be a source of comfort
and visual delight. It can have a calming effect. All
symmetry is repetition.

Sometimes, repetition is qualified by variation,
natural or industrial. Stone pavements provide the
delight of repetition as well as variation, recognition
as well as new experience. Repetitive simplicity
with a twist of imprecision comforts and tickles
our senses at the same time. Less than perfect
repetition, more of the same, but slightly different,
constitutes the beauty of collections.

Repetition is not necessarily generated by addition;
it can be created by subdivision of a large body into
small units. This is the case with many building
facades. Conceptually, they are broken down, rather
than built up, in identical units. Practically, it is the
other way around. Repetition and variation may be a
question of viewing distance.

116

Figure 116
Cobblestones
Opposites repetition and
variation together create an
intriguing pattern.

Figure 117
Nationalbanken,
The Danish central bank
Design Arne Jacobsen /
Dissing+Weitling, 1965/70
The repetition of facade
elements has a calming
effect while the lack of
approachability signifies
safety.

Figure 118
Gottesacker graveyard,
Christiansfeld, Denmark
Gottesacker is German for
God's acre.
Repetition as equaliser.

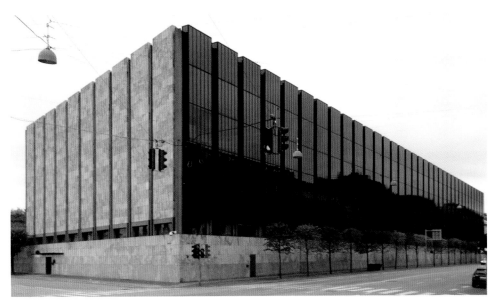

117

118

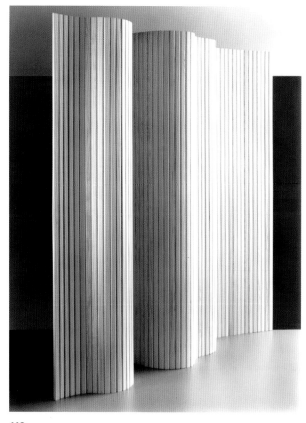

119

Figure 119
Screen 100 room partition, 1936
Design Alvar Aalto
Manuf. Artek, Finland
As the repeated units become smaller and grow in number, paradoxically, the overall design gets closer to the power of oneness.

Figure 120
The Sackler Crossing, Royal Botanic Gardens, Kew, UK, 2006
Design John Pawson
Repeated flat granite planks and bronze uprights serve as deck and balustrade.

Figure 121
Royal Hotel, Copenhagen, Denmark, 1960
Design Arne Jacobsen
Sometimes repetition is not generated by addition, but by subdividing a large body into small, identical units.

120

121

Tatami are inches thick modular straw mats that cover the floors in traditional Japanese homes. A tatami forms a double square measuring ca. six feet on the long side; the exact measures vary with the locality.

Tatami are placed close to each other on the floor, where they serve as an insulating surface on which Japanese used to live their indoor life – some still do. The occupants wear tabi, socks with separation for the big toe, and zori, sandals with a thong, instead of their outdoor footwear that is left at the entrance to the house. The occupants sit directly on the tatami and eat at a low table. At night they take out their futon mattresses from a cupboard, lay them on the tatami and sleep close to the floor.

The rooms in traditional houses are dimensioned to hold a certain number of tatami: two, four, four and a half, six, eight, ten, twelve, and so on. Tatami are placed in configurations where four corners never meet.

Apart from determining the size and shape of traditional rooms, tatami measures are reflected in the elements of walls and ceilings. Along with the practical function tatami provide rooms with a definite sense of order. Today, many Japanese families who otherwise live western style keep one tatami room to be used for special occasions.

Room sizes in real estate ads in Japan are still indicated with the tatami as unit of measurement: a 12 tatami room is ca. 20 m^2.

Figure 122
Tatami in use

Figure 123
Tatami patterns
Tatami meet in Ts. Four corners never meet.

122

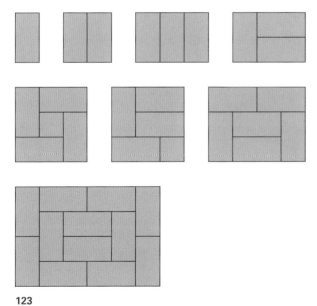

123

The sphere, the ball, is the ultimate simple object. *Die Liebe zur Geometrie*, the love of geometry, is strong. The sphere has one surface, no edges, and no corners. Also, a sphere has the optimal volume/surface ratio. No other solid body has so much volume with so little surface. The sphere's capacity for rolling makes it a natural prop in sports and games.

The principle behind the *superellipse*, a marriage between rectangle and ellipse, was conceived by French mathematician Gabriel Lame (1795–1870) who generalised the equation for the ellipse. Later, Danish author and designer Piet Hein named and marketed the *superellipse* – and invented the three-dimensional *superegg*.

124

Figure 124
**Vacuum Jug Kugel of stainless steel, 1985
Design Ole Palsby
Manuf. Alfi, Germany**
The jug's favourable volume/surface ratio supports the insulating property.

Figure 125
**Flower Pot, 1968
Design Verner Panton
Manuf. 1968, Louis Poulsen, Denmark
Manuf. 2010, &tradition, Denmark**

Figure 126
**Pastil, 1967
Design Eero Arnio
Manuf. Adelta International, Germany**

125

126

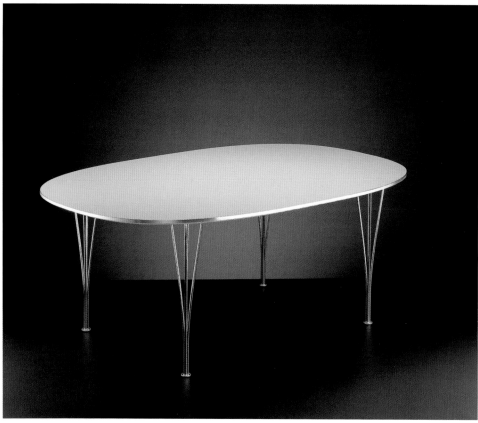

127

Figure 127
Superellipse table, 1968
Design Piet Hein /
Bruno Mathsson
Manuf. Fritz Hansen,
Denmark
Not a circle, not a rectangle,
the superellipse combines
advantages of both.

Figure 128
The Egg, hanging chair,1957
Design Nanna & Jørgen
Ditzel
Manuf. 1957, R. Wengler,
Denmark
Manuf. 1957, Pierantonio
Bonacina, Italy

128

The term *wabi-sabi* frequently pops up in discussions about simplicity in traditional Japanese material culture. The concept evades precise verbal description. Precision is not part of the wabi-sabi tradition. In fact, evasiveness seems to be an essential part of the philosophy. But, however elusive, wabi and sabi may be approached by a few characteristics.

Wabi and sabi were originally two separate concepts that in the fourteenth century were paired and gradually took a new meaning. Today the two words most often appear hyphenated. Originally, wabi dealt with living in isolation, mostly a philosophical attitude, and sabi originally dealt with something worn down, an aesthetic ideal of artefacts.

The contemporary meaning of wabi-sabi is perhaps best captured by comparing wabi-sabi with modernism as suggested by Leonard Koren in *Wabi-Sabi for Artists, Designers, Poets & Philosophers* (1994).

Both modernism and wabi-sabi deal with artifacts and both originated as reactions to other aesthetic directions: nineteenth century classicism and eclecticism, and sixteenth century and earlier Chinese perfection, respectively. Both modernism and wabi-sabi are abstract and non-representational ideals defying ornaments not integral to structure.

The differences between modernism and wabi-sabi are essentially that modernism is sophisticated, seamless, technologically advanced, geometric, and public, while wabi-sabi is primitive, imperfect, natural, organic, and private.

Koren, Leonard
Wabi-Sabi for Artists, Designers, Poets & Philosophers
Stone Bridge Press, Berkely, CA, 1994

Koren pinpoints the simplicity connection:

The simplicity of wabi-sabi is probably best
described as the state of grace arrived at
by a sober, modest, heartfelt intelligence. The
main strategy of this intelligence is economy of
means. Pare down to the essence, but don't
remove the poetry (1994, p72).

Industrial design is typically influenced by
modernism while arts and crafts feature qualities
similar to those celebrated by wabi-sabi.

129

Figure 129
Thrown Bowl, 1973
Design Bernard Howell
Leach
Small bowl with grey glaze
and white brush decoration.
From the W. A. Ismay Studio
Ceramics Collection at
York Art Gallery.
Wabi-sabi?

130

Figure 130
Cylinda Line, 1964/67
Design Arne Jacobsen
Manuf. Stelton, Denmark
Not wabi-sabi.

Like scientists, designers stand on the shoulders of each other, even if they are not always ready to admit so. The father of modern Danish furniture design, Kaare Klint, took the past seriously and taught his furniture students how inspiration should be taken from already existing furniture types ready for refinements by reduction of superfluous elements. The result of this procedure was later dubbed *the functional tradition*, a label that does not immediately reveal that it was not the function per se, but rather the aesthetic expression of the function, that interested the designers. The exercise was as much a matter of aesthetics as of functionality.

Several of the greatest achievements of Danish furniture designers are developments of well-known furniture types originated in other countries. One common denominator of these new designs is simplicity. After taking inspiration in many places the designers cut to the bone and put the functional elements on show. Occam's Razor at work. Among the foreign chair types adopted for further development by Danish designers are Chinese chairs, Chippendale chairs, Latin slat back chairs, Windsor chairs, and cantilever chairs.

Figure 131
Cover of Mobilia Design Magazine featuring the exhibition *Offspring – Danish Chairs with Foreign Ancestors*, 1983
Design Henry Anton Knudsen
Editor/curator Per Mollerup
The cover illustration demonstrates the Chippendale pedigree of the Red Chair by Kaare Klint.

Offspring

Danish Chairs with Foreign Ancestors
Danske stole med udenlandske aner

mobilia

No. 315/316 1983

1:5

131

132

133

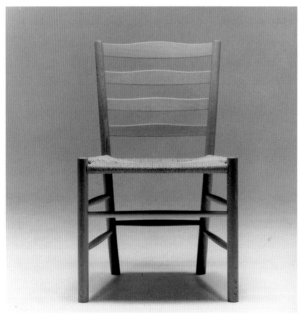

134

Figure 132
Latin slat back chair, acquired
in Italy, 1920s

Figure 133
Church chair with shelves for
hymnbook and hat, beech,
1936
Design Kaare Klint
Manuf. Fritz Hansen,
Denmark

Figure 134
The church chair without
shelves, 1936
Design Kaare Klint
Manuf. Fritz Hansen,
Denmark

Figure 135
Chair no. 39, beech, 1947
Design Børge Mogensen
Manuf. FDB, Denmark

Figure 136
Diagonally oriented chair,
beech, 1962
Design Mogens Lassen
Manuf. Fritz Hansen,
Denmark

135

136

Ethics – Simplicity for conscience

Like functionality and aesthetics, ethics may concern qualities inherent in the design. However, ethics goes a step further and involves limitation or rejection of artefacts.

Ethics deals with ideas about what is right and what is wrong. This issue allows for a fair number of ideas rooted in many ideologies, religions, political and other convictions. These ideas are externally anchored to the degree that the believers transcend themselves and respond to some external authority. However, the idea may also be purely idiosyncratic: simplicity is good for me. Rooted in age-old traditions, churches are better organised and more physically present than other movements concerned with ethics. This has affected the balance of this chapter.

Richard Bach
The simplest things are often the truest.

Winston Churchill
A vocabulary of truth and simplicity will be of service throughout your life.

Edsger Dijkstra
Simplicty is a prerequisite for reliability.

Dalai Lama
Simplicity is the key to happiness in the modern world.

Henry David Thoreau
Our life is frittered away by detail... Simplify, simplify, simplify! ... Simplicity of life and elevation of purpose.

Leo Nikolayevich Tolstoy
There is no greatness where there is no simplicity, goodness, and truth.

Jesus delivered Christianity's killer argument
against earthly wealth when he declared it easier
for a camel to pass through the eye of a needle
than for a rich man to enter the kingdom of God
(Matthew 19:24). However clear, this parable
hasn't been totally successful on a pragmatic level.
Well heeled Christian people have no problems
in bending Jesus's message. Some of them fancy
Christian fundamentalists relaying a narrow gate
in Jerusalem called *The Eye of the Needle* through
which a camel could just barely squeeze. No matter
what, organised religion has not seen Matthew's
parable as a prohibition of churches massing robust
fortunes.

Many Christian churches and monasteries are
ambiguous when it comes to dealing with wealth.
In some situations, they translate the ban on wealth
into qualitative terms, for instance when offering
strictly spartan seating to worshippers. Also, some
monasteries and churches are extremely austere,
while other Christian churches are stuffed with
rich ornamentation and valuable works of art.
Some churches present a delicate balance between
austerity and ostentatious wealth.

Other religions than Christianity recommend
material simplicity. They also seem to suggest
that restrain in earthly possession is conducive to
attention to, and acceptance by, their God.

Other ethical, including political, considerations keep
people from gathering earthly wealth. Socialists
and others with a social conscience take the middle
sector of the socialist freedom–equality–fraternity
dictum seriously.

Figure 137
Pews, Moritzkirche,
Augsburg, Germany,
2008–2013
Design John Pawson
Why is seating more frugal
in churches than in concert
halls? Is uncomfortable
seating conducive to serious
worshipping? Does it prevent
churchgoers from snoozing
during the service?

137

The Shakers, or *the Shaking Quakers*, were religious worshippers with a highly developed material culture characterised by simplicity, utility, and beauty. They lived and practised their religion in eastern and midwestern communities in North America from the middle of the eighteenth century. Their official name was *The United Society of the Believers in the First and Second Appearance of Christ*. The Shaker name referred to a state of ecstasy reached through their communal dances. At some point, that part of their worship was abandoned.

The first Shakers were dissidents from the British Anglican church. Under the spiritual leadership of Mother Ann Lee, nine Shakers emigrated to North America in 1774. When the movement was at its zenith in the middle of the nineteenth century the Shakers numbered around 6,000 members in 19 settlements in Maine, New Hampshire, Massachusetts, Connecticut, New York, Ohio, and Kentucky. In the twentieth century, the movement declined. At the beginning of the twenty-first century, only a few Shakers remain living in the Sabbathday Lake settlement in Maine.

The Shakers were utopians and lived in celibacy with segregated sexes. New members were converts and orphans from the outside world. The Shakers shared belief, work, and ownership. They also believed in equality among sexes, in confession, and in pacifism.

The Shakers developed an outstanding material culture. They designed their tools and surroundings, from the smallest utensils to houses and carefully planned villages. In the process they made practical inventions such as the flat broom and the circular saw and took a patent for a washing machine. After fulfilling their own needs, the Shakers would sell their products to the world.

Figure 138–139
Building details, Canterbury
Shaker Village, Canterbury,
NH, USA

138

139

Shaker design is informed by functional, ethical, and aesthetic considerations. The Shakers had a clear vision that their tools should be useful, and that austerity and beauty should go hand in hand with utility. *The Shakers had their eyes in Heaven while their feet remained on Earth*, said Paul Rand.

Shaker design gave rise to a small industry of furniture, boxes, baskets, and more. The products have survived as a never-forgotten legacy. Among others, Danish designers have taken inspiration from the Shakers and in some cases taken up Shaker furniture for further development.

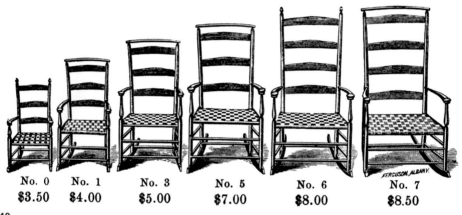

WORSTED LACE SEATS.

| No. 0 | No. 1 | No. 3 | No. 5 | No. 6 | No. 7 |
| $3.50 | $4.00 | $5.00 | $7.00 | $8.00 | $8.50 |

140

The Shakers are sometimes compared with the Amish. However, two apparent differences separate these religious groups. One is that the Amish never developed a material culture that can be likened with that of the Shakers. Another difference is that the Shakers welcomed modern technology, the Amish don't. In modern times, the Shakers own automobiles, while the Amish still use their buggies, small lightweight carriages drawn by a single horse.

Figure 140
Shaker rockers, 1876

Figure 141
Slanting slat back Shaker chair, ca. 1840–50
Canterbury, NH, USA

Figure 142
Shaker table, 1947
Design Børge Mogensen
Manuf. 1947, FDB, Denmark
Manuf. 2010, Fredericia Furniture, Denmark
When designing this table Danish furniture designer Børge Mogensen followed the Shaker trail and made no secret of his inspiration.

141

142

Church of the Light is a small concrete edifice designed by Tadao Ando and built in 1989 for a protestant congregation in Ibaraki, a suburb to Osaka. A cruciform cut out of the concrete wall behind the altar justifies the name of the church. The cross extends from wall to wall and divides the wall into four rectangles.

Church of the Light is located in a hilly residential area dominated by one-family houses. In contrast to the often-publicised photos taken immediately after the construction was completed, Church of the Light does not appear isolated, but submits, partly covered by trees, to the surroundings. To find Church of the Light, one must know exactly where it is.

The church is a concrete box pierced by a freestanding concrete wall in an angle of 15 degrees, which gives the nave an intriguing five-sided shape and provides space for an entree in the cut off area. The light from the cross cut into the wall dominates the austere interior of the nave. More than any stained-glass complexity the simple cruciform gives the room its character, provides an ever-changing experience of light, and symbolically dedicates the space to its religious purpose. The pews add a resource-saving dimension to the singular simplicity of the edifice: they are made of the wood used for scaffolding. Simplicity including massive absence, but no poverty, characterises Church of the Light in a way congenial with its spiritual function.

Ten years after the church was finished, an independent annex was added to house a Sunday school.

Figure 143
Church of the Light, Osaka,
Japan, 1989
Design Tadao Ando
Photo: Mitsuo Matsuoka

143

For millennia, philosophers, religious movements, and individuals have developed ideas about voluntary restraint in consumption and possessions. Thinkers such as Diogenes, Epicure, Gandhi, and Thoreau practised and propagated limited consumption and possessions. The Greek city state of Sparta left a legacy of parsimony and restraint still living in the adjective, *spartan* (written with lower-case initial). In modern times, these ideas have been reinforced by the emerging conscience about the state of the Earth. Population and waste increase while natural resources decrease and nature is threatened. *The world, if it has a future, has an ascetic future*. Arkady in Bruce Chatwin: *Songlines,* (1987) 1998, p133.

These concerns point to downsized consumption, the natural quantitative response. But sometimes this reduction translates into qualitative changes.

In the USA, a great number of websites, magazines, books, and organisations suggest ways readers, members, and followers can simplify their lives. Some of these promotions appear more driven by business than by idealism. The clutter of the relevant websites gives a first warning.

Quantitative considerations can clearly lead to simplicity in design. But the influence can also work in another direction, and that is the gospel of simplicity in design: Good, simple design suggests restraint in possession. A couple of Poul Kjærholm PK22 chairs suggest restraint in space and time. *First,* they do not look good in cluttered surroundings. *Second,* owners take care of them hoping to keep them for the remaining part of their life.

We take delight in things;
We take delight in being loosed from things.
Between these two delights, we must dance our lives.
Philip Harnden in *Journeys of Simplicity*, a collection of the belongings of 40 authors and artists, among them Gandhi, Marcel Duchamp, Henry David Thoreau, and Robert Piersig.

Harnden, Philip
Journeys of Simplicity
SkyLight Paths Publishing, Woodstock, NY, 2003

Danish author and designer Piet Hein suggested that people who own more than eight things, are in fact owned by their things:

The Tyranny of Things
I am trying to rule over ten thousand things
which I thought belonged to me.
All of a sudden a doubt takes wings:
Do they ... or could it be...?
A hardhanded hunch in my mind's ear rings
from whence such suspicion may stem:
that if you possess more than just eight things
then you are possessed by them.

Figure 144–145
PK22 chair, 1955
Design Poul Kjærholm
Manuf. 1955, E. Kold Christensen, Denmark
Manuf. 2010, Fritz Hansen, Denmark
Sometimes simple design suggests restraint in the surroundings.

144

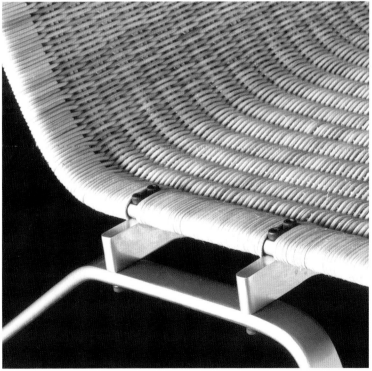

145

For people dreaming of a simple life in solitude close to nature or just questing simplicity in the everyday, *Walden*, by Henry David Thoreau (1851), serves as a bible. Thoreau wrote *Walden* during a sojourn in a self-built cabin at Walden Pond in the woodland near Concord, Massachusetts. The land was owned by Thoreau's friend, Ralph Waldo Emerson, whom he often visited during his stay. The sojourn lasted two years and two months; the book's cult status has lasted for one and a half centuries.

Walden is an ode to nature and to downsizing consumption and possession. When Thoreau uttered his often quoted *Simplicity, simplicity, simplicity*, he talked about reduction. According to Thoreau, man has four material needs: clothes, shelter, food, and heat, and all four needs deal basically with heat. We could do with less of all four categories than we normally do. In his forest cabin Thoreau would prove that; he spent next to nothing on housing, clothing, and heating.

Thoreau's interest for nature and for simple living met in his belief in transcendentalism where God, humankind, and nature are one and the same thing.

Critics have questioned Thoreau's natural human, pointing to his daily visits to Concord and his dependence on weekly foraging visits to his mother who lived two miles away. These details have not discouraged Thoreau's proselytes. *Walden* is mentioned and cited in, and has inspired, numerous other books.

Thoreau, Henry David
Walden
Illustrated Modern Library,
New York, 1937

Figure 146
Henry David Thoreau
***Walden*, 1851**
Original title page, illustration
by Thoreau's sister Sophia
Thoreau's ode to nature and downsizing serves as a bible to people dreaming of a simple life in solitude.

WALDEN;

OR,

LIFE IN THE WOODS.

By HENRY D. THOREAU,

AUTHOR OF "A WEEK ON THE CONCORD AND MERRIMACK RIVERS."

I do not propose to write an ode to dejection, but to brag as lustily as chanticleer in the morning, standing on his roost, if only to wake my neighbors up. — Page 92.

BOSTON:
TICKNOR AND FIELDS.
M DCCC LIV.

146

Simplicity in visual communication

In the three previous chapters we have discussed simplicity in product design with a few digressions into the graphic design of watch dials. Many of the concepts and principles dealt with apply to graphic design as well as to three-dimensional design. Even then, the differences including a number of issues applying exclusively to communication design, are substantial and interesting enough to warrant a specific treatment of visual communication.

Literature about simplicity in visual communication traditionally treats simplicity as were it exclusively a question of aesthetics, about minimalism. This is not the case. Simplicity in graphic form can be conducive to clarity, which facilitates perception and cognition. This is a functional issue. Further, simplicity in graphic form can be an issue of ethics.

Ralph Waldo Emerson
It is a proof of high culture to say the greatest matters in the simplest way.

Ernest Hemingway
My aim is to put down in paper what I see and what I feel in the best and simplest way.

Ludwig Wittgenstein
What can be said at all can be said clearly; and whereof one cannot speak thereof one must be silent.

Simplicity and its opposites, complexity and complication, are ubiquitous qualities. We find them everywhere, in nature, and in the human-made world, including visual communication.

In visual communication, form and content are closely intertwined, but not necessarily in a straightforward manner. Complex and complicated matters are – sometimes – communicated in simple ways, and simple matters are – often – communicated in complicated ways.

The means used for visual communication are writing and a battery of non-verbal elements including overall arrangement. Writing is composed of letters, which in turn are signs for sounds that stand for meanings. Non-verbal elements stand for meanings and guide the reader's attention.

Graphic design is not necessarily an innocent servant that merely lets the meaning pass untouched from sender to receiver. The graphic form can manipulate: weaken, strengthen, or flavour the message. The visual tone of voice may say as much as the words and may be instrumental in the way the intended message is noticed, read, understood, sympathised with, and accepted or rejected.

Clarity – and beyond that understandability viz. functionality – is one major motive for simplicity in communication. Another major motive is the aesthetic pleasure of simplicity as minimalism. A third motive for graphic simplicity can be a wish to send signals of ethical austerity. These three motives correspond to the three motives for simplicity in product design. Also, as in other design, simplicity in visual communication may be the result of limited available technology.

Figure 147–148
Simplicity in visual communication comes in many forms.

Figure 147
Logo for
Oslo Airport Gardermoen,
1996
Design Designlab

Figure 148
Paul Rand
A Designer's Art, 1985
Design Paul Rand
A great book in a great, simple design.

OSL✈

147

Without specific formal limitations and without the challenge of play, both teacher and student cannot help but be bored. The product may take the form of a superficial (but sometimes "professional looking") literal translation of the problem, or of a meaningless abstract pattern or shape, which, incidentally, may be justified with enthusiasm but often with specious reasoning.

Similarly, there are badly stated problems in basic design that stress pure aesthetics and free expression without any restraints or practical goals. Such a problem may be posed in this fashion: arrange a group of geometric shapes in any manner you see fit, using any number of colors, to make a pleasing pattern. The results of such vagaries are sometimes pretty, but mostly meaningless or monotonous. The student has the illusion of creating great art in an atmosphere of freedom, when in fact he is handicapped by the absence of certain disciplines which would evoke ideas and make playing with those ideas possible, work absorbing, and results interesting.

The basic design problem, properly stated, is an effective vehicle for teaching the possibilities of relationships: harmony, order, proportion, number, measure, rhythm, symmetry, contrast, color, texture, space. It is an equally effective means for exploring the use of unorthodox materials and for learning to work within specific limitations.

To insure that theoretical study does not end in a vacuum, practical applications of the basic principles gleaned from this exercise should be undertaken at the proper time (they may involve typography, photography, page layout, displays, or symbols).

The student learns to conceptualize, to associate, to make analogies; to see a sphere, for example, transformed into an orange, or a button into a letter, or a group of letters into a broad picture. "The pupils," says Alfred North Whitehead, "have got to be made to feel they are studying something, and are not merely executing intellectual minuets."[4]

If possible, teaching should alternate between theoretical and practical problems, and between problems with tightly stated "rules" imposed by the teacher and problems with rules implied by the problem itself. But this can happen only after the student has been taught basic disciplines and their application. He then is able to invent his own system for "playing the game." "A mind so disciplined should be both more abstract and more concrete. It has been trained in the comprehension of abstract thought and in the analysis of facts."[5]

There are many ways in which the play principle serves as a basis for serious problem-solving, some of which are discussed here. These examples indicate, I believe, the nature of certain disciplines and may suggest the kinds of problems that will be useful to the student as well as to the teacher of design.

4. Alfred North Whitehead, *The Aims of Education* (New York, 1949), 21.

5. Ibid, 24.

The Romanesque church Badia de Fiesole exhibits surprising playfulness on every inch of its facade. (c. 850)

191

148

While all kinds of graphic design contain some kind of information, *information graphics* is a term used about a special type of graphic design that deals with visual explanation. Information graphics is a subcategory of information design, which also includes three-dimensional design. Objectivity, accuracy, and clarity are qualities of special importance in information graphics. Clarity follows from simplicity, so much that the two terms are often used synonymously. In information graphics unclear information is anathema, in some situations clear or unclear information can be a question of life or death. Unclear road signs, unclear lifeboat instructions, and unclear information on medicine packaging are points in case.

Wayshowing including environmental signage is a field where clarity is often compromised. Worn-out signs, signs with too little colour contrast, signs with too small type, badly organised signs, signs covered by foliage or other signs, contradicting signs, illogical signs, and too many signs are phenomena well-known to travellers. Simplicity should be rule number one in good wayshowing: enough is enough.

Data visualisation includes pie charts, bar charts, line charts, and many other graphic displays comparing quantities, locations, and connections. News media, business reports, and other media use them for understanding, insight, attraction, and memorability. All these intended results depend on simplicity and clarity. Nevertheless we often see seducingly colourful displays that are more conspicuous, complex, and complicated than clear. Marie Neurath, one of the originators of Isotype* picture tables, gave a rationale, which – simple as it is – applies to all good data visualisation:

> *Everything which would not help you understand the meaning, or which would confuse you, is left out. Colours are used only to help make the meaning clearer, never simply as decoration. This means that every line and every colour in these pictures has something to tell you.***

Information graphics include several categories of graphic design, among them:
– cartography
– data visualisation
– document design
– financial information
– interactive design
– human–machine communication
– medical information
– news graphics
– product graphics
– road signs
– slide presentations
– technical illustration
– traffic and transport information
– timetables
– user instructions
– warning signs
– wayshowing
– web design

* Isotype, International System Of TYpographic Picture Education, also called *The Vienna Method of Pictorial Statistics*, is a special approach to data visualisation developed in Vienna 1925–34 by Otto Neurath and Georg Arntz.

**Quoted from Burke, Christopher; Kindel, Eric; Walker, Sue (Eds.) *Isotype: Design and contexts 1925–1971* Hyphen Press, London, 2013

149

150

Figure 149–150
Wayshowing Copenhagen
Airport, 1989
Design Designlab
In wayshowing as in other
branches of information
graphics simplicity is a major
concern.

After having finished writing *Les Misérables*,
French author Victor Hugo reportedly left Paris
for the countryside. After some time in pastoral
surroundings, Hugo wanted to know how his book
had fared. He sent his publisher a cable consisting
of one character, a question mark. Having read
the cable carefully, the publisher answered with
another cable of equal magnitude and spirit: an
exclamation mark.

While this story may be apocryphal, it gets
to the point of our discussion of simplicity in
communication. To benefit from this kind of minimal
correspondence, interlocutors must share a code
and a frame of reference. The receiver must share
the culture of the sender and see the message in the
right context.

The code in the anecdote is trivial. The publisher
and the author both know the general meaning of a
question mark and an exclamation mark.

Both messages are coloured by the context, the
situation in which they are sent and received. The
publisher understands the author's interest in
knowing the fate of his book. The author has an
idea of possible replies to his inquiry. Publisher and
author share frames of reference.

Our everyday is filled with short messages where we
know the code and read them in a certain context. A
stylised picture of a drinking glass on a parcel sent
by mail means *handle with care*. A similar glass
seen on a sign in the airport means *bar*.

Codes, systems of signs shared by a group, can be
used to shorten and thereby simplify messages. As
long as the sender and the receiver are in the same
ballpark and agree about the code, about what
means what, codes can be highly effective and save
time and space. It is faster to Morse and receive an
SOS than a full *Save Our Souls*. If the receiver does
not understand the code, it complicates, rather than
simplifies, the communication.

Figure 151
DR TV logo, Denmark, 1994
Design Designlab
Designers of identification
marks for TV-stations enjoy
considerable freedom as
long as the marks are easily
distinguishable from similar
marks used by competing
stations. When the author's
studio did the station
identification for the Danish
national television in 1994,
the intention was to make it
simple. Too simple, many felt.

Figure 152
YLE 1 logo, Finland, 1996
Design Liisa Kallio
Finnish television took up the
idea of the non-present figure
of one and cut it down to the
most descriptive half of the
surroundings. Improvement
by simplification.

Codes are not restricted to letters, but can in principle include any *sign* in the semiotic meaning of that word. Siren signals, uniform distinctions, and piste colours are all non-verbal codes. Dentists, physicians, stockbrokers, bookmakers, and many other professions and trades use special codes that facilitate fast and reliable recording and communication. Such codes can also – intentionally or not – contribute to mystifying a trade. That points to another function of codes: secret storage and transmission of messages. Codes may shorten and make messages simpler to understand for those who know the code and more complicated for those who don't.

151

152

Skilled card players, musicians, conjurers, and athletes practice their discipline with as little not needed effort as possible. So do many skilled graphic designers. When showing distinction they husband the use of effects and stick to the just-noticeable difference.

The just-noticeable or smallest necessary difference implies that graphic designers emphasise with modesty. If everything is emphasised, nothing is emphasised. That logic is universal; it applies to signage systems, to train schedules, and to all other GUIs, graphic user interfaces.

In terms of typography, the principle of the just-noticeable difference implies that graphic designers do not emphasise a header by location, and different font, and size, and weight, and italics, and capitals, and colour, and underlining, at the same time. One, perhaps two, of these command variables will do. Enough is enough, but enough is necessary. Remember redundancy.

Several writers have warned against verbose messages:

The art of writing is to refrain.
Paul Rubow

Style is the art of omission.
Somerset Maugham

The secret of being a bore is to say everything.
Voltaire

To be a good writer you must kill your darlings.
Iris Murdoch

As to the adjective: when in doubt, strike it out.
Mark Twain

The more bloody good stuff you cut out, the more bloody good your novel will be.
Ernest Hemingway

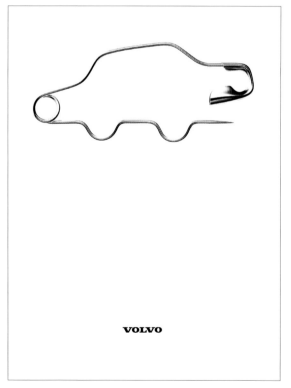

VOLVO

Figure 153
Volvo ad, 1996
Design Dentsu Y&R, Japan
Volvo, Sweden
Some ads draw attention by conspicuous restraint. Sometimes, a whisper goes further than a shout.

153

Le superflu, cette chose necessaire
Voltaire

Voltaire hardly had redundancy in mind when he
talked about the necessity of the superfluous.
Nevertheless his adage suits redundancy perfectly
well – writer's serendipity? In communication
redundancy stands for repetition that reduces
the probability of misunderstanding. Too much
redundancy makes reading boring and is a
waste of energy. Too little redundancy makes the
message vulnerable to omissions, errors, and
misunderstanding.

154

The need for redundancy in communication weakens
the rule that more elements mean less simplicity.
As far as understanding of a message is concerned,
a certain spillover may simplify perception and
cognition. Behind this apparent contradiction stands
the difference between quantity-simplicity and
quality-simplicity.

Written language is redundant on several levels,
visually as well as verbally. In a typical newspaper
article, letters, words, sentences, and sometimes
sections can be removed without loss of meaning
for the educated reader. On the other hand, some
redundant information increases the probability that
the readers will understand the message as intended
by the sender. Messages without redundancy are
vulnerable to any kind of error or noise.

Redundancy in communication is a matter of
subjectivity. Readers with a certain background
may see a certain piece of information as
highly redundant, while readers with a different
background may not find it understandable. The
location of the borderline between too little and
too much redundancy is a matter of the sender's
Fingerspitzengefühl, situational awareness.

Symmetry, patterns, and style involve redundancy
for aesthetic reasons.

Figure 154
Visual redundancy
enables recognition and
understanding under less
than perfect conditions.

The parameters of simplicity described in the Basics part of *Simplicity: A Matter of Design* also apply to graphic design – with some qualifications.

The number of elements clearly plays a role. The basic rule is that more elements mean less simplicity. However, this rule is partially amended by the need for redundancy – repetition that facilitates understanding. There is no sharp limit between useful and useless redundancy. This involves several factors, including the capabilities of the intended receivers. The watch with strokes is simpler to read than the naked watch dial (see p17). The following section relates documents that become simpler when longer.

The variety of the elements included in a work of graphic design can play a significant role. More variety can make the appearance less simple while making reading simpler if used to emphasise structure, or it can make reading less simple if it is used for pure decoration. Different fonts used for different kinds of content may simplify reading. Different fonts used for the same type of content may complicate reading. The basic principle is that variety in form should be used to show variety in meaning. The watch with figures is simpler to read than the watch with strokes, or without figures or strokes.

Structure plays a decisive role for the simplicity of a graphic work. Logical relations, pattern, sequence, and order are clues. Structure, or visual organisation, is a key tool in information graphics, graphic design aiming at understanding and knowledge rather than feelings and persuasion. A train timetable with exact information and good typography fails if the user cannot find the needed item because of bad overall structure.

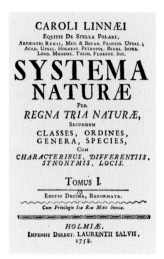

155a

How complex or simple a structure is depends critically upon the way in which we describe it.
Herbert Simon
The Science of the Artificial
MIT Press, Cambridge, MA, 1969

Figure 155
Cover and spread from Carl Linnaeus aka Carl von Linné:
Systema Naturæ, **1735**
An important, scientific structure visualised in a well-structured display.

155b

Documents, on paper or screen, are frequent sources of distress. Receivers find them unnecessarily complex and complicated. They are too long and too difficult to understand. The causes behind this state of affairs may be several. Some relate to the document design, some relate to the language. This distinction is not completely clear.

When politicians now and again declare war on red tape and promise less paperwork to citizens and employees, they traditionally envisage shorter documents stripped of superfluous verbiage. These politicians have a biased focus on quantity while documents would often be simpler if they were longer. This apparent contradiction originates from confusing two levels of simplicity. One is the immediate appearence, shorter documents look simpler – quantity-simplicity. The other is the use. A longer document with better explanation may be simpler to use – quality-simplicity. In document design fewer elements do not necessarily mean more simplicity in use. The opposite is very often the case.

When it comes to simplification of documents the Simplification Centre in England discerns between *optimisation* and *transformation*.

Rob Waller and Simplification Centre, England, consult on simplification of documents. They have published a number of papers on this topic including *Simplification: what is gained and what is lost*, that has informed this section. Interested readers should download the paper from www. simplificationcentre.org.uk

The table below is adapted after *Simplification: what is gained and what is lost.*

Optimisation			Plain language editing
			Clear typographic design
			Access structure
Transformation	Reduction	*It gets shorter*	Omission
			Distillation
			Abstraction
	Amplification	*Clearer but longer*	Learning helps
			Glossing
			Visualisation
	Stratification	*Broken up*	Layering
			Drill down
			Routeing
	Reframing	*Rebuilt from scratch*	Reconstruction
	Personalisation	*Focus on relevance*	Customisation
			Helplines and advisers

Optimisation includes the standard factors that should dignify any document: easily read typography and easily understood language. The Simplification Centre talks about *hygiene factors*.

Transformation changes documents in more drastic ways.

Reduction includes what many would understand as real simplification. Omission leaves out not needed parts, distillation reduces to the essential, and abstraction takes out a part for immediate use, while the remaining part is delivered on demand.

Amplification involves additional elements. Learning helps explain issues in different ways, e.g. by adding questions. Glossing stands for explanatory marginalia. Finally, visualisation includes graphics that explain the structure of a problem.

Stratification divides the text into recognisable layers or types that allow readers to structure the reading.

Layering uses typographic variation to distinguish different layers of explanation. Drill-down links higher level explanations directly to lower level explanations on other pages. Routeing gives explicit information how to navigate through a document: 'Go to (25)'.

Reframing implies a complete reconstruction of the content which is deconstructed into pieces for assembling in a new and more comprehensible way.

Personalisation can take the form of customised documents where text blocks are gathered according to the receiver's profile. The means of last resort may be a help desk or a personal adviser that helps the reader through the document.

A sender can just send a message in whatever shape comes to mind. Then the receiver will have to sort out what the sender really meant. Alternatively, the sender can take the time to structure the message in a short, clear way. In this case, the receiver will have less work to do. The argument for choosing this distribution of work between sender and receiver grows in importance as the audience becomes larger. One sender's efforts benefit many receivers.

Shortness of a message is a question of quantity. It is conducive to simplicity in appearance, a matter of aesthetics. If the meaning is not lost in reduction, shortness may also be conducive to simplicity in explanation, a question of clarity, which means functionality. The danger of shortness in communication is that the message becomes vulnerable because of too little redundancy.

Shortness in form may take its toll in longer preparation for the sender: the paradox of simplicity. All senders of factual information know that a short form may involve long preparation. To make a simple and clear timetable, tax declaration form, telephone directory, or user guide takes time.

In a letter to a friend, Blaise Pascal wrote: *I made this letter larger than usual because I lack the time to make it short.* Similar quips are attributed to Mark Twain, Marcel Proust, and Voltaire, and to any number of journalists reporting to their editor.

Mark Twain is also reported saying that it took him two days to write 30 pages, and 30 days to write two pages.

Asked by a journalist how long he took to prepare a ten-minutes speech, US President Harry Truman answered: *Two hours.* When asked how much time he needed to prepare a speech of one hour, Harry Truman answered: *One hour, but if the speech takes two hours, I can make it right away.*

Figure 156
Poster for exhibition about architect Mogens Lassen, 1972
Design Henry Anton Knudsen
However simple in appearance, good graphic design may involve considerable work.

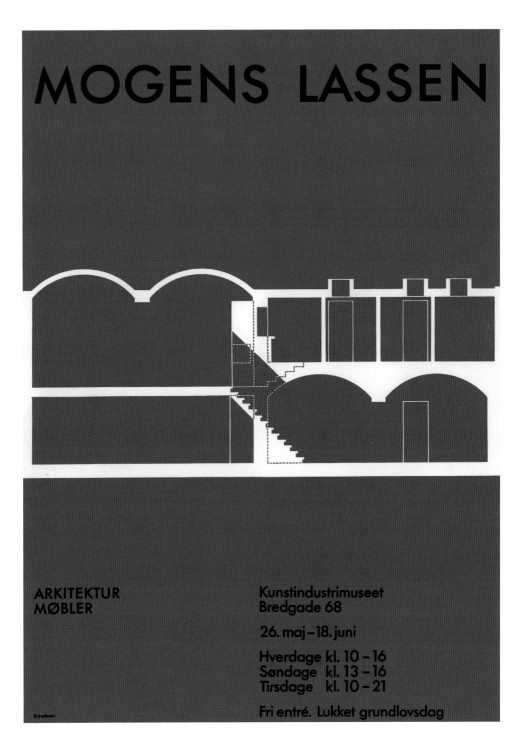

156

All graphic design depends on colour contrast by definition. In addition to making messages discernible, colour is used for separation and guidance, for conveying meanings, and for decoration.

Colour is the fastest working graphic means. Readers identify colour a long time before they recognise specific shapes. This quality comes in handy when colour is used to convey meanings such as those we know from navigation at sea: green for starboard, red for port side. This is also the case when we look for a car rental company in the airport: yellow for Hertz, red for Avis, orange for Budget, green for Europcar.

Many trades and activities use time-honoured colour codes conventionalised by use or agreement. Red stands for danger. In martial arts the obis (sashes) can have up to ten different colours to indicate the wearer's fitness for fight.

Colour-blind persons may have difficulties with some colour codes, unless they are backed up by position such as practised by traffic lights: red at the top, yellow in the middle, green at the bottom.

157

Examples of well-known colour codes.					
Traffic	Stop		Go	Wait	
Navigation	Port side		Starboard		
Meeting room	Occupied		Vacant		
Hotel room	Don't disturb		Please clean		
Skiing	Difficult	Easy	Very easy		Very difficult
US Highways		Motorway	Primary route		
Accounting	Deficit				Surplus
Tap water	Hot	Cold			
EU customs	Something to declare	EU citizen	Nothing to declare		
Theatre	Full				
Politics*	Left wing	Right wing	Greens		
*USA doesn't follow this principle: Democrats are blue, Republicans red.					

158

Figure 157
Traffic sign, Melbourne
Red stands for danger.

Figure 158
Traffic signal, New York
The colour coding is
supported by the spatial
arrangement: red/top, yellow/
middle, green/bottom.

To graphic designers, a universal picture language that can be understood intuitively by anybody independently of their language, educational, and cultural background is a tempting – and utopian – ambition. Some designers have offered proposals for comprehensive visual sign systems to simplify communication.

159

An early elaborate picture 'language' is Isotype International System Of TYpographic Picture Education, conceptualised by Otto Neurath in Vienna in 1936 and designed by Georg Arntz. Neurath's aim was to describe economic and social issues to the lay population by the use of graphic symbols. Whereas Isotype was designed to disseminate knowledge, pictograms as we know them today are primarily designed to enable informed action.

To remember simplified images is better than to forget accurate numbers.
Otto Neurath

Pictograms are pictorial signs created as an alternative to written language. The idea is that pictograms are faster to read and that they can be understood by illiterate people as well as people with diverse language and cultural backgrounds. To enable universal understanding, pictograms should be *motivated* – in contrast to being *arbitrary*. They should be immediately recognisable and understandable by the intended audience. Also, pictograms should be *conventionalised,* well known due to standardisation and widespread use. If one of these two conditions – motivation and conventionalisation – is not met, the other condition becomes more important. Unfortunately, many pictograms are not immediately understandable, and we do not have one all pervasive standard (see p44).

Figure 159
Isotype pictogram, 1930s
Concept Otto Neurath
Design Georg Arntz

The best pictograms depict the service or situation they represent in a straightforward manner. The picture of a knife and fork is in the western world immediately understood as *a place where you can eat*. Other pictograms are less straightforward. That a picture of a standing gentleman means *male toilet* is not immediately understandable. Such pictograms must be learned before they work.

Figure 160
AIGA pictograms
Design AIGA, USA
AIGA, the Professional Association for Design, has in collaboration with the US Department of Transportation designed a set of 66 pictograms characterised by great simplicity. The pictograms are available on the Web, free of charge.

160

The proper understanding of pictograms depends on the users' culture, their background and knowledge, as well as the context in which the pictograms are seen. Sometimes, pictograms shown side by side give a clue to each other. Perhaps the users do not know all the pictograms, but those that they know may hint how the others should be understood.

Branding, development, and maintenance of a brand, simplifies the exchange of merchandise for seller and buyer. In its contemporary meaning, a brand is a combination of a core, its presentation to the world, and the resulting image. The core can be a company, a product, a service, an event, or something else.

The purpose of commercial branding is to sell more at a higher price. The means is to establish an emotional relation to prospective buyers.

To the seller, branding means an effective way to make the company and its products or services known, respected, and to create customer loyalty. To the buyer, branding helps orientation in a marketplace with its plethora of companies, products, and services.

Branding functions as a conceptual shorthand, a simplification. The trademark and, perhaps, a dominant colour serve as a psychological convenience that helps consumers focus their knowledge and feelings about the brand. Consumers observe and recognise hundreds of trademarks and read them as beacons in the marketplace. Based on communication and experience they consider the brand – represented by the trademark – as a promise.

Graphic design plays a major role in branding, notably in the design of trademarks, but also in the total *mise-en-scène* of companies, products, and services. Some companies do well with rather complex brandmarks. However, the simplicity of some of the world's strongest brandmarks is striking.

Figure 161
Nike logo, 1971
Design Carolyn Davidson

Figure 162
Apple logo, 1977
Design Rob Janoff

Figure 161–162
The two strongest logos in the world? That depends, but strong enough to work, without colours, without company name, and without obvious semantic connection with company or product.

161

162

The visual identity programme designed by Otl
Aicher and Sepp Landsbeck for FSB, Franz Schneider
Brakel, a German manufacturer of building fittings,
stands out in a number of ways. None of the several
remarkable corporate identities designed by Otl
Aicher – Lufthansa, the 1972 Olympic Games in
Munich, ERCO, Bulthaupt – is simpler. Otl Aicher,
prolific German designer, was a great simplifier, but
an even greater systematiser. In his design for FSB
simplicity is the defining quality.

The FSB pictorial trademark grabs attention by
its striking simplicity. How can so little be so
distinctive? The trademark depicts a door handle, or
rather the concept of a door handle. Otl Aicher got
the inspiration for the graphic door handle in Haus
Wittgenstein in Vienna. When philosopher Ludwig
Wittgenstein built this stately home for his sister,
he also designed the building fittings, among them
door handles with two different grips, one for each
side of the door. The door handles are made of metal
rods and consist of a minimal number of parts. FSB
eventually took up Wittgenstein's door handle for
production after a necessary adjustment.

Otl Aicher delivered more than graphic design. He
inspired a corporate philosophy.

Figure 163
Haus Wittgenstein door
handles, 1928
Design Ludwig Wittgenstein

Figure 164
Identity elements, 1985
FSB Brakel, Germany
Design Otl Aicher /
Sepp Landsbeck.

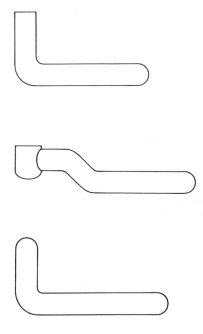

163

164

Much literature on web simplicity concentrates on the number of elements. Authors advise designers to remove what is not needed. However, there is more to simplicity in visual communication than reducing the number of elements (see p34, p154).

Variety is a second important factor. Variety can be a great simplifier when it is used to signal variety in meaning by separating different types of information. Variety can, in principle, involve any type of graphic effect, location, colour, typeface, size, and more. If variety is used for pure decoration, it reduces simplicity and increases clutter.

For large bodies of information, logical structure can be the most important factor for creating simplicity. Order and method are the key to good wayshowing in large quantities of information. A clear structure may compensate for a large amount of elements.

Structure concerns both the structure of the single page and the structure of the total site. What is immediately apparent? What must be found? The choice between broad and deep structure is central. Some pundits hold that there should never be more than six choices on a page. This implies a deep solution. Other information specialists prefer as many parallel choices as possible. This implies a broad solution.

Web users can handle a large number of menu items if they are presented in a sensible way. A rolling list of 52 North American states is preferable to a deep menu starting with Eastern, continuing with Midwestern, and ending with Western states.

How special simplicity should be depends on the presumptive users. While websites with timetables for trains should be easily understandable for everyone including first-time users: general simplicity, websites monitoring the trade on the stock exchange should primarily be understandable for professionals: special simplicity.

Figure 165
Google home page
The home page of Google is a homage to simplicity. Deep solution, general simplicity.

Figure 166
Jacob Nielsen's home page
In his much acclaimed book, *Designing Web Usability,* Jacob Nielsen stresses simplicity as the core virtue of web design.
Jacob Nielsen's own home page is stuffed with information. The simple structure combined with the lack of not needed variety makes navigation easy in spite of a great number of elements. Broad solution, general simplicity.

165

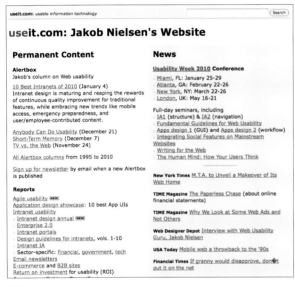

166

Graphic clutter is not a normal requirement of functional communication. However, we cannot rule out the possibility that ambiguity and lack of clarity in some situations by some senders and some readers can be seen as valuable graphic qualities.

Different types of communication have different demands on clarity. Objective messages with factual details intended to create understanding and knowledge require greater clarity than subjective messages intended to evoke feelings. As a rule, first aid instructions and scientific papers need more clarity than record covers, fashion ads, and tabloids.

Cluttered design with many layers and several more or less blurred and maimed typefaces may result from the designer's urge to capture the *Zeitgeist* as well as from the designer's desire to play all bells and whistles.

Clutter also happens as a natural consequence of the technology available to the trade. The medium makes the message. Computer software offers possibilities that, however outlandish, will sooner or later be deployed.

Finally, cluttered design may of course reflect the designer's inability to craft a body of information in a straightforward manner.

Intentionally no illustration

Heretical postscript

Everything should be made as simple as possible, but not simpler.
Albert Einstein

Should simplicity always be preferred to complexity and complication? Do complexity and complication have no merits whatsoever?

Simplicity has its limitations. These are reflected in language by such words as *simplism, simplistic, simpleton*, and *simp*. The noun *simplism* and the adjective *simplistic* refer to the tendency to oversimplify an issue by ignoring relevant features. In a similar vein, a *simpleton* or *simp* is a person lacking intelligence and common sense.

Complication is the defining element in many sports, epitomised by obstacle races and orienteering. To complicate wayfinding without making the mission impossible is the amusing purpose of mazes. Milton Glaser's iconic rebus (mental obstacle race), I♥NY, is much more memorable than the same message said in plain words.

Figure 167
New York strapline, 1977
Design Milton Glaser
Complication is the point of rebuses. A rebus is a visual pun where letters are represented by pictures. Sometimes a rebus may effectively support memory. Why else would we remember, repeat, and emulate Milton Glaser's iconic strapline?

Index

Sources

A Place in Time
The Shakers at Sabbathday Lake, Maine
Pocket Paragon Books, Jaffrey, NH, 2006

Abrahamsen, Povl
Den danske enkelhed
Christian Ejlers' Forlag, Copenhagen, 1994

Aicher, Otl; Kuhn, Robert
Greifen und Griffe
FSB Franz Schneider Brakel, Brakel, Germany, 1987

Anderson, Chris
The Long Tail: Why the Future of Business is Selling Less of More
Hyperion, New York, 2006

Antonelli, Paola
Humble Masterpieces
The Museum of Modern Art, New York, 2006
Thames & Hudson, London, 2006

Berger, Arthur, A.
What Objects Mean: An Introduction to Material Culture
Left Coast Press, Walnut Creek, CA, 2009

Berthoz, Alain
Simplexity: Simplifying Principles for a Complex World
Yale University Press, New Haven, CT, 2012

Blaser, Werner
Mies van der Rohe, Lehre und Schule, Principles and School
Birkhäuser, Basel, 1977

Bono, Edward de
Simplicity
Viking, London, 1998

Botton, Alain de
The Architecture of Happiness
Hamish Hamilton, London, 2006

Brandes, Uta (Ed.)
Dieter Rams, Designer: Die leise Ordnung der Dinge
Steidl Verlag, Göttingen, 1990

Brändle, Christian et al.
Sportdesign
Edition Museum für Gestaltung Zürich, Zurich, 2004

Burke, Christopher; Kindel, Eric; Walker, Sue (Eds.)
Isotype: Design and contexts 1925–1971
Hyphen Press, London, 2013

Burkhart, François; Franksen, Inez (Eds.)
Design: Dieter Rams &
Gerhardt Verlag, Berlin, 1980

Calza, Gian C.
Japan Style
Phaidon, London, 2007

Die Shaker
Die Neue Sammlung, Munich, 1974

Doblin, Jay
One Hundred Great Product Designs
Van Nostrand Reinhold Company, New York, 1970

Emlen, Robert P.
Shaker Village Views
University Press of New England, Hanover, NH, 1987

Engstrand, Johanna; Furuland, Maria (Eds.)
Minimalism
Feierabend, Berlin, 2003

Furuyamo, Masao
Ando: The Geometry of Human Space
Taschen, Cologne, 2006

Harlang, Christoffer, et al. (Eds.)
Poul Kjærholm
Arkitektens Forlag, Copenhagen, 1999

Harnden, Philip
Journeys of Simplicity.
SkyLight Paths Publishing, Woodstock, NY, 2003

Sources

Heller, Steven; Fink, Anne
Less is More: The New Simplicity in Graphic Design
North Light Books, Cincinnati, OH, 1999

Hillman, David; Gibbs, David
Century Makers
Weidenfeld & Nicholson, London, 1998

Index: 100 Stories of design to improve life
INDEX: Award, Copenhagen, 2010

Iwamiya, Takeji; Takaoka, Kazuya
Katachi, Japanese Sacred Geometry
Pie Books, Tokyo, 2005

Jennings, Jason
Less is More: How Great Companies Improve Productivity without Layoffs
Portfolio, New York, 2002

Jenson, Scott
The Simplicity Shift: Innovative Design Tactics in a Corporate World
Cambridge University Press, Cambridge, UK, 2002

Kahney, Leander
Jony Ive: The Genius Behind Apple's Greatest Products
Portfolio Penguin, London, 2013

Klemp, Klaus; Ueki-Polet, Keiko (Eds.)
Less and More: The Design Ethos of Dieter Rams
Gestalten, Berlin, 2009

Kluger, Jeffrey
Simplexity: Why Simple Things Become Complex (and How Complex Things Can Be Made Simple)
Hyperion, New York, 2008

Koren, Leonard
Wabi-Sabi for Artists, Designers, Poets & Philosophers
Stone Bridge Press, Berkely, CA, 1994

Kulvik, Barbro
The DNA of Design
Fiskars Corporation, Helsinki, 2007

Levy, Stephen
The Perfect Thing
Simon & Schuster, New York, 2006

Logan, William Bryant
The Tool Book
Workman Publishing, New York, 1997

Loos, Adolf
Ornament und Verbrechen, 1908
Reprint Vienna, 1930

Loos, Adolf
Spoken into the Void: Collected Essays 1897–1900
MIT Press, Cambridge, MA, 1982

Lowell, Sophie
Dieter Rams: As Little Design as Possible
Phaidon, London, 2011

M&C Saatchi
Brutal Simplicity of Thought
Ebury Press, New York, 2011

Maeda, John
The Laws of Simplicity
MIT Press, Cambridge, MA, 2006

Marzona, Daniel
Minimal Art
Taschen, Cologne, 2004

Meader, Robert F. W.
Illustrated Guide to Shaker Furniture
Dover Publications, New York, 1972

Mente, Boyé Lafayette De
Elements of Japanese Design
Tuttle Publishing, Tokyo, 2006

Merell, Floyd
Simplicity and Complexity: Pondering Literature, Science, and Painting
University of Michigan Press, Ann Arbor, MI, 1998

Sources

Meyer, James (Ed.)
Minimalism
Phaidon, London, 2000

Minimalisme, Minimalism
Feierabend Verlag oHG, Berlin, 2003

Mollerup, Per
Marks of Excellence: The History and Taxonomy of Trademarks
Phaidon, London, (1997) 2013

Mollerup, Per
Collapsibles: A Design Album of Space-Saving Objects
Thames & Hudson, London, 2002

Mollerup, Per
Wayshowing>Wayfinding: Basic & interactive
BIS Publishers, Amsterdam, 2013

Mollerup, Per
Data Design: Visualising quantities, locations, connections
Bloomsbury Academic, London, 2015

Morse, Edward S.
Japanese Homes and their Surroundings
Dover, New York, 1961

Mostaedi, Arian
Minimalist Spaces
Carles Broto & Josep Mª Minguet, Barcelona, 2003

Muller, Charles R.; Rieman, Timothy D.
The Shaker Chair
University of Massachusetts Press, Amherst, MA, (1984) 1992

Müller-Brockmann, Josef
Grid systems / Raster systeme
Verlag Niggli, Heiden, CH, (1981) 1996

Murray, Stuart
Shaker Heritage Guidebook: Exploring the Historic Sites, Museums & Collections
Golden Hill Press, Spencertown, NY, 1994

Neumeier, Marty
Zag: The #1 Strategy of High-Performance Brands
New Riders, Berkely, CA , 2007

Nielsen, Jacob
Designing Web Usability
New Riders, Berkely, CA, 2000

Norman, Donald A.
The Design of Everyday Things
Basic Books, New York, (1988) 2002

Norman, Donald A.
Emotional Design: Why we love (or hate) everyday things
Basic Books, New York, 2005

Norman, Donald A.
The Design of Future Things
Basic Books, New York, 2007

Norman, Donald A.
Living with Complexity
MIT Press, Cambridge, MA, 2010

Ott, John Harlow
Hancock Shaker Village
Shaker Community Inc., Berkshire County, MA, 1976

Papanek, Victor
Design for Human Scale
Van Nostrand Reinhold, New York, 1983

Pawson, John
Minimum
Phaidon, London, 1996

Pawson, John
Themes and Projects
Phaidon, London, 2002

Pearce, Joseph
Small is still beautiful
ISI Books, Wilmington, DE, 2006

Sources

Powell, Richard R.
Wabi Sabi Simple
Adams Media, Avon, MA, 2005

Rand, Paul
A Designer's Art
Yale University Press, New Haven, CT, 1985

Rathgeb, Markus
Otl Aicher
Phaidon, London, 2006

Rudofsky, Bernard
The Kimono Mind: An informal Guide to Japan and the Japanese
Victor Gollancz, London, 1966

Rudofsky, Bernard
Sparta/Sybaris
Residenz Verlag, Vienna, 1987

Sarnitz, August
Adolf Loos 1870–1933: Architect, Cultural Critic, Dandy
Taschen, Cologne, 2003

Schwartz, Barry
The Paradox of Choice: Why More is Less
Ecco, New York, 2004

Segall, Ken
Insanely Simple: The Obsession That Drives Apple's Success
Portfolio/Penguin, New York, 2012

Shea, John G.
The American Shakers and Their Furniture
Van Nostrand Reihold Company, New York, 1971

Sheridan, Michael
Room 606: The SAS House and the Work of Arne Jacobsen
Phaidon, London, 2003

Siegel, Alan; Etzkorn, Irene
Simple: Conquering the Crisis of Complexity
Twelve, New York, 2013

Simon, Herbert
The Science of the Artificial
MIT Press, Cambridge, MA, 1969

Sommar, Ingrid
Den skandinaviska stilen
Valentin, Stockholm, 2003

Sôshitsu XV, Sen
The Spirit of Tea
Tankosha, Tokyo, 2002

Sprigg, June
By Shaker Hands
Alfred A. Knopf, New York, 1975

Sprigg, June
Shaker Design
Whitney Museum of American Art, New York, 1986

Sprigg, June; Larkin, David
Shaker: Life, Work, and Art
Cassell, London, 1988

Stephensen, Magnus; Stephensen, Snorre
Brugsting fra Japan
Arkitektens Forlag, Copenhagen 1969

Sudjic, Deyan
Cult Objects
Paladin Books, London, 1985

Sudjic, Deyan
John Pawson Works
Phaidon, London, 2000

Sudjic, Deyan
The Language of Things
Alan Lane, London, 2008

Sudjic, Deyan
B is for Bauhaus: An A-Z of the Modern World
Particular Books, London, 2014

Sources

Sunstein, Cass R.
Simpler: The Future of Government
Simon & Schuster, New York, 2013

Taschen, Angelika (Ed.)
Minimal Style: Exteriors, Interiors, Details
Taschen, Cologne, 2006

Tenner, Edward
Why Things Bite Back: Technology and the Revenge of Unintended Consequences
Vintage, New York, 1997

Thoreau, Henry David
Walden
Illustrated Modern Library, New York, 1937

Trout, Jack, with Rivkin, Steve
The Power of Simplicity: A Management Guide to Cutting Through the Nonsense and Doing Things Right
McGraw-Hill, New York, 1999

Tufte, Edward R.
The Visual Display of Quantitative Information
Graphic Press, Cheshire, CT, 1983

Tufte, Edward R.
Envisioning Information
Graphic Press, Cheshire, CT, 1990

Tufte, Edward R.
Visual Explanation
Graphic Press, Cheshire, CT, 1997

VandenBroeck, Goldian, (Ed.)
Less is More: An Anthology of Ancient & Modern Voices Raised in Praise of Simplicity
Inner Traditions, Rochester, VT, 1991

Waldrop, M. M.
Complexity: The Emerging Science at the Edge of Order and Chaos
Penguin, London, 1994

Waller, Rob
Simplification: what is gained and what is lost
Simplification Centre, UK, no year
Downloadable from www.simplificationcentre.org.uk

Watches from IWC
International Watch Company, Schaffhausen, CH, 1997

Wheatley, Margaret J.; Kellner-Rogers, Myron
A Simpler Way
Berrett-Kohler Publishers, San Francisco, CA, 1996

Zabalbeascoa, Aatxu; Marcos, Javier Rodriguez
Minimalisma
Editorial Gustavo Gili, Barcelona, 2000

Zednicek, Walter
Adolf Loos
Eigenverlag Walter Zednicek, Vienna, 2004

Zumthor, Peter
Thinking Architecture
Lars Müller Publishers, Baden CH, 1998

1   Safety Pin by Haragayato / CC BY-SA 3.0
2   K Helmer-Petersen
4   Azuma house / CC BY-SA 3.0
5   Ole Mathiesen
6   Ole Mathiesen
7   Ole Mathiesen
8   Ole Mathiesen
9   INDEX: Design to Improve Life®
10 Apple
11 RIM
12 INDEX: Design to Improve Life®
13 2CV-1956-Caen by Rundvald / Public Domain
14 Ben Olson
15 The Milkmaid / Google Art Project / CC BY-SA 3.0
19 Lynette Zeeng
20 Fiskars
21 Thonet
22 Thonet
23 Mark Hyman
24 Concorde by Christian Kath / CC BY-SA 3.0
25 Dyson
26 Woldbye & Klemp
33 Getty Images
34 Concorde / CC BY SA 3.0
35 Klos
36 Tata Nano im Verkehrszentrum des Deutschen Museums by High Contrast CC BY-SA 3.0
37 Citroën DS front 20080126 / CC BY-SA 3.0
38 Citroën DS rear 20080126 / CC BY-SA 3.0
40 DS interieur kleine. Licensed under Public Domain via Wikimedia Commons
41 Submarine periscope / Licensed under Public domain via Wikimedia Commons
42 Getty Images
43 Per Mollerup
44 BMW
45 BikeHUD
46 Garmin HUD
47 Per Mollerup
48 Bastian Andersen
50 Citroën Typ H 1981 grey vl TCE by Stahlkocher / CC BY SA 3.0
51 2008-04-14 Chrome-Vanadium Wrenches by Ildar Sagdejev / CC BY-SA 3.0
53 Surgical Instruments / CC0 1.0 Universal Public Domain Dedication
54 Lynette Zeeng
55 SONY Cyber-shot DSC W530 by Joydeep / CC BY SA 3.0
56 B&O
57 Tokyobike

58   Soldatenmesser 08-2 by Francis Flinch / CC BY 3.0

59   Bahco

60   Louis Schnakenburg

62   Ducati 748 Studio by Stefan Krause / CC BY-SA 3.0

63   Piaggio

64   Piaggio

65   Braun

66   Braun

67   Bang & Olufsen

68   Olivetti Valentine. Folletto at it.wikipedia / CC SA 3.0

69   Zanotta

70   Apple

71   Apple

72   Apple

73   Rohloff-nabe / CC BY-SA 3.0

74   Shimano xt rear derailleur by C. Corleis / CC BY-SA 3.0

75   Louis Schnakenburg

76   Louis Schnakenburg

77   BMW

78   Viking

79   Woldbye & Klemp

80   Artek

81   Normann Copenhagen

82   Yann Libessart/MSF

83   DonaldJudd IMJ by Talmoryair / Licensed under GFDL via Wikimedia Commons

84   Farnsworth House 2006 by Carol M. Highsmith / Licensed under Public domain via Wikimedia Commons

85   Therme Vals facade, Vals, Graubünden, Switzerland - 20090809, von Micha L. Rieser. Lizenziert unter Creative Commons

86   Looshaus Vienna June 2006 546 von Gryffindor / CC BY 2.5

87   Wien Hietzing, St.-Veit-Gasse 10 - 1 by Wolfgang J. Kraus. Licensed under Public domain via Wikimedia Commons

88   Braun

89   Cubus

90   Braun

91   Vitsoe

92   Seagram Building by Tom Ravenscroft / CC-BY-2.0

93   Vitra

94   K Helmer-Petersen

95   K Helmer-Petersen

96   Herman Miller

97   Børge Schiang

98   Pennsylvania Railroad steam engine PRRS1, Licensed under Fair use of copyrighted material in the context of Raymond Loewy via Wikipedia

99   Harley Earl and "The Y Job" / CC BY-SA 2.0

Other books by Per Mollerup include:

Marks of Excellence: The History and Taxonomy of Trademarks, 1997
A revised and expanded edition was published in 2013.

Collapsibles: A Design Album of Space-Saving Objects, 2002

Wayshowing: A Guide to Environmental Signage, 2005

Brandbook: Branding, Feelings, Reason, 2008
(in Danish).

PowerNotes: Slide presentations reconsidered, 2011
Downloadable from http://hdl.handle.net/1959.3/191214

Wayshowing>Wayfinding: Basic & Interactive, 2013
Revised and expanded version of *Wayshowing: A Guide to Environmental Signage,* 2005

Data Design: Visualising quantities, locations, connections, 2015

168

Figure 168
Tungen/ The Tongue, 1985
Design Arne Jacobsen
Manuf. Howe, Denmark
Tungen was designed for
Munkegårdsskolen, a Danish
primary school. Production
was reassumed in 2013.